THE
ESCAPE
BOOK

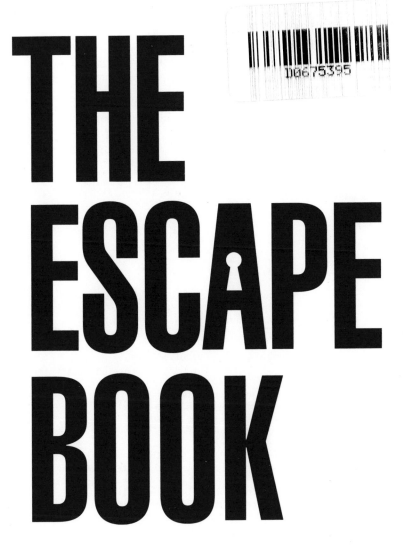

Acknowledgements

Thank you to Óscar and Alicia for locking me inside a room and not letting me out. To Laia, Greta and Rita for being locked up with me each day. To Montse for helping me find the codes. Thanks also to Ferran for checking they were the right ones. And thanks to Irene and Javier for giving me somewhere to put them.

Brimming with creative inspiration, how-to projects and useful information to enrich your everyday life, Quarto Knows is a favourite destination for those pursuing their interests and passions. Visit our site and dig deeper with our books into your area of interest: Quarto Creates, Quarto Cooks, Quarto Homes, Quarto Lives, Quarto Drives, Quarto Explores, Quarto Gifts, or Quarto Kids.

© 2018 Quarto Publishing plc.
Text © 2017, 2018 Ivan Tapia

This edition published in 2020 by Chartwell Books,
an imprint of The Quarto Group,
142 West 36th Street, 4th Floor, New York, NY 10018, USA
T (212) 779-4972 F (212) 779-6058 www.QuartoKnows.com

First published in Spanish in 2017 by Lunwerg

First published in the UK in 2018 by Aurum Press,
an imprint of The Quarto Group,
The Old Brewery, 6 Blundell Street
London N7 9BH United Kingdom
www.QuartoKnows.com

Ivan Tapia has asserted his moral right to be identified as the Author of this Work in accordance with the Copyright Designs and Patents Act 1988.

Every effort has been made to trace the copyright holders of material quoted in this book. If application is made in writing to the publisher, any omissions will be included in future editions.

A catalogue record for this book is available from the British Library.

ISBN: 978-0-7858-3892-0

10 9 8 7 6 5 4 3 2 1

Typeset in ITC New Baskerville
Illustrations and Design by Run Design

Printed in Singapore COS062020

THE ESCAPE BOOK

Can you escape this book?

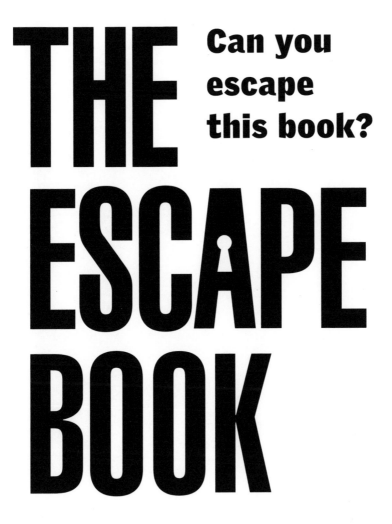

Ivan Tapia

CHARTWELL
BOOKS

READ THIS FIRST

During an escape-game experience, participants must test their intelligence and creativity, along with their skills of observation and analysis, to solve a puzzle.

The Escape Book doesn't explain how someone solves a puzzle; the reader is the main character. Since the chapters of the book are jumbled up, the reader must solve the puzzles if they wish to know where to continue reading.

How do I play along with this book?
Read each chapter until you reach this padlock symbol:

Once there, just like Candela Fuertes – the main character trapped in the maze – you will have to go back and solve the puzzles that have appeared over the course of the chapter. Each time you solve a puzzle, the number that you arrive at will indicate the page from which you can continue the story.

What happens if I can't solve the puzzles?

Don't worry. At the end of each chapter, you will find a page number, where you will find clues that will help you to achieve your goal.

You decide whether you want to use one clue, all the clues or no clues at all. It's up to you to set the difficulty level of this book. You can also skip ahead or back as you see fit.

I hope you're able to escape from *The Escape Book* with Candela Fuertes.

Good luck!

THE BEGINNING

Candela has 56 minutes left to live.

TICK-TOCK TICK-TOCK TICK-TOCK TICK-TOCK

On the floor of a room lies the body of a young woman; her eyes are closed. Is she dead? Her chest rises and falls weakly. Up... down... up... She's alive. The skirt of her long dress is still rolled up; we can see her tights, which are black and laddered. Her mane of auburn hair is wild and messy. Her skin is too white, a contrast with her red lips.

Up... down... up... The emergency light is too dim. A soft and persistent sound resonates in the dark room. It's the sound of the turbines that started up a moment ago to suck out the deadly gas that had emerged from the sprinklers hidden in the roof minutes earlier.

Up... down... up... The woman opens her eyes. She tries to blink, but can't close her eyes. She tries to talk, but her mouth does not open. One second, two seconds. Finally, she does blink. A single tear makes her mascara run. Time stops, but as hard as she tries to move, her body remains motionless.

She has only 56 minutes left.

The woman focuses her energy on breathing. In... out... in... She cannot move. She is disoriented. She tries to speak, but cannot. She is afraid. In... out... in... She tries again, and her lips move.

'I'm... Candela Fuertes.' Her voice is a whisper. Movement slowly returns. She turns her head to one side and looks at the space only implied by the darkness. In... out... in... She turns her head to the other side with a gentle thud. It hits the wall softly, but just enough to kick-start the neurons. The light in her brain switches back on; everything else is still in the shadows.

8

Candela Fuertes is a journalist. Twenty-eight years old. Many stories to tell, some to keep quiet and none she could ever forget. The future of millions of people who do not know her depends on this woman. And she only has a few minutes left to live.

She already knows where she is and how she got there. What she doesn't know is how much time has passed. But she does know that if she isn't able to get up, her future will end – and with it, the world as we know it. She begins to move, muscle by muscle. At a pace halfway between that of a silkworm and a Komodo dragon, she manages to shift into a sitting position.

'How much time has passed?'

Now on all fours, she touches the ground. Searching... searching... She finds a stopwatch. It's attached to her wrist and indicates that she has 54 minutes to die.

'Or to live.'

Leaning against the wall in the dim light, Candela gets up. She has no idea how she will get out. She's locked in. She must escape, but it will not be easy. She already knew this when she entered the Daedalus, the labyrinth of death created by Castian Warnes.

TICK-TOCK TICK-TOCK TICK-TOCK TICK-TOCK

First it was just another case, then it was *the* case, and now it is her life. Three months ago, she began investigating Castian Warnes – the big finance man, admired by his enemies and feared by his friends. The man capable of changing the course of the world economy with a single tweet. Candela scoured over photos, forums, comments, gossip columns, biographies, press statements and blogs until she ended up stumbling upon the existence of the Daedalus in a TV interview. The magnate was talking about his 'infallible' security system, with controls that bordered on the criminal.

'Mr Castian, what would happen if an intruder were to enter the Daedalus?' asked the host.

Very simple. A lethal gas would end his life in 60 minutes if he did not inject the corresponding antidote in time. Only I can get out of it.

Castian delivered his answer with a smirk. At home, sitting on her futon in front of the television, Candela could not believe it. This man repulsed her, but she couldn't stop watching.

Worse still was the magnate's answer when asked by the interviewer about the questionable legality of the system. Looking straight into the camera, Warnes answered:

The intruder would go to the cemetery and I would go to court. But I can assure you, it would be worth it. I have the best lawyers.

Then, with that characteristic smile, he challenged anyone who might want to do so to put the Daedalus to the test. Candela shuddered.

I can assure you that the Daedalus is impassable. I am so sure of it that I can tell you where you will find the entrance: just behind the table in my office in Ferulic Castle. If anyone wants to visit, be my guest.

Carmela felt like she'd been challenged – and she was tempted.

'I'll get you, arrogant swine.'

Just as she'd finished her journalism degree, Candela witnessed one of her best friend's grandmothers being evicted. The woman had lost her flat thanks to a bank that had no qualms about casting her out into the street. A whole life spent caring for her tiny home, only to end up in her grandson's spare room. She died two months later – a heart attack, said the doctors. Her grandson thought it was heartbreak. Candela had helped her friend to confront the bank. They lost. Candela had learnt a lesson. She had grown up and decided to dedicate her life to unmasking those who hurt ordinary folk.

There is nothing that Candela likes more than revealing murky stories, unpaid taxes, dark pasts or dodgy dealings.

Six years later, and now an investigative reporter, Candela is the light that illuminates the world in the era of communication.

Although not for much longer if she can't escape. She has 53 minutes left.

TICK-TOCK TICK-TOCK TICK-TOCK TICK-TOCK

Little by little, her disorientation dissipates and Candela's heart beats with force once again. Escape. Advance. Don't delay. Her head hurts and it costs her to breathe; that's the venom, surely? If Castian Warnes said that only he could exit the maze, it's because there is an exit. Her bag has disappeared and with it her mobile phone. She is alone.

'Think, Candela. Think.'

Think. How can she? It's difficult to see, because the emergency light doesn't reach all the corners of the room. Candela moves towards the wall on her left and blindly feels it. Step by step, hand by hand. Eyes closed, all senses tense. The first wall. Corner. Nothing. Next wall. Step by step, hand by hand. Something different… Wood? Candela stops and opens her eyes. She retraces it with her fingers. A door. It feels like the door she entered through. It's closed.

Candela explores the full room. Another change of material. Metal? It's more than a metre wide. Candela doesn't breathe. She touches. Smells. Listens. She can feel the expectancy ahead. Hand by hand, finger by finger. A button. She doesn't know what will happen if she pushes it. She doesn't have time. All or nothing. She closes her eyes tightly and…

Click.

The room is illuminated. Around six by six metres of absolute nothingness. A bare space. A void. No furniture, pictures, tables. Nothing. Only anodyne grey walls. And the silence, now the turbines have stopped.

'Think, Candela. Think.'

She looks closely at the metallic door. On the right side, there is a numeric keypad. She pushes a random key. Beep. Then another. Beep. And another. Beep. And another. Buzz. The door is still closed.

'I need a three-digit combination.'

She knows there's a possibility. She's scared. What will there be on the other side of that door? How much time will Warnes allow her to live?

Candela feels like she's being watched. Eyes burning into the back of her head. She puts her hair up into a bun and tucks her skirt into her belt so she can make a run for it if she needs to. She looks at the gate ahead of her. She already knows what lies on this side. Death. There's only one way to go. Forward. Now, with the light on, she looks closely again at the room. The two doors – the one through which she entered, and the other through which she'll exit. And in the walls, she finds metal plates she hadn't felt with her hands before. They're covered in bolts. One plate to the left, and three smaller ones to the right.

'So, is that the secret?'

The game has just started, and Candela must open the door of the first room if she wants to live. There are 52 minutes left to play.

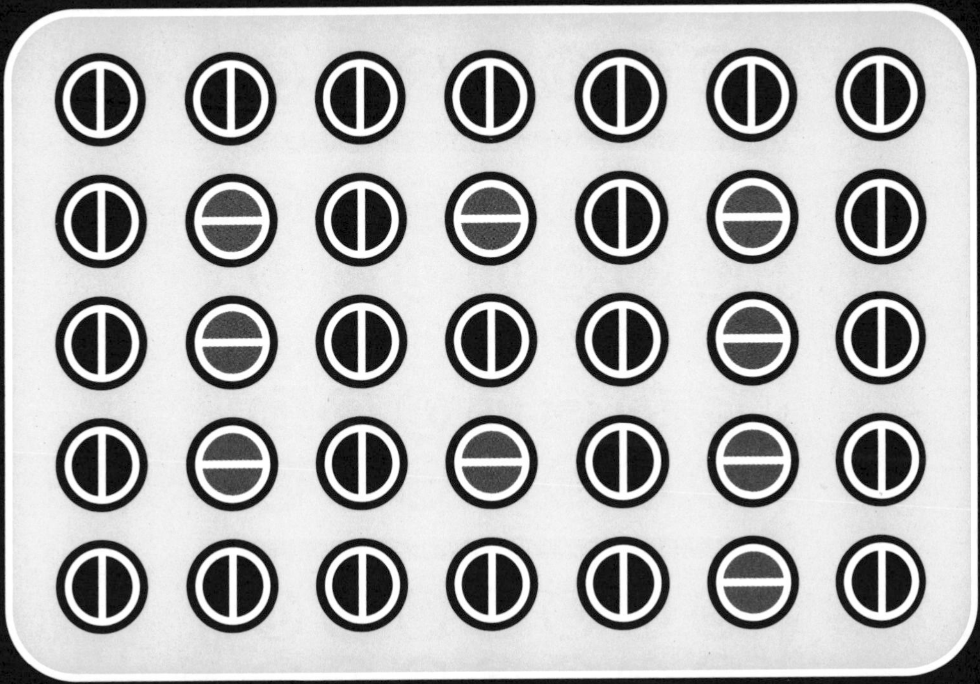

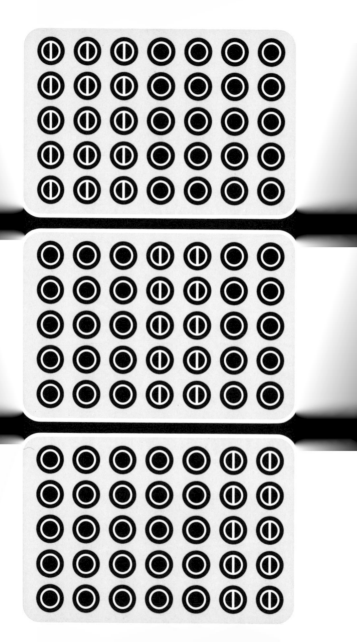

On this page, the puzzle still hasn't been solved.
Find the key to know where to continue.
If you need to, consult the clues on page 143.
Write the key here so you can remember it later on.

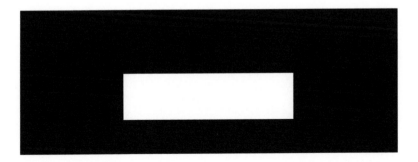

CANDELA SOLVES THE PUZZLE OF THE FINAL PAINTING

She has 14 minutes left to live.

TICK-TOCK TICK-TOCK TICK-TOCK TICK-TOCK

She sees it! Candela approaches the numerical keypad of the final painting as fast as she can, and quickly inputs the code she thinks she has found in the painting. It doesn't work. Did she get it wrong? She hasn't managed to type in the right code, her fingers are stiff. She has 14 minutes left. There's no time to lose. She swears and mentally goes over the steps she's followed so far. She's unsure of everything now. She cannot be sure of anything.

The password is correct, it has to be. She tries again, slowly and very carefully. Her fingers are shaking, but this time she does not make any mistakes.

The lamp, that had been visible from the hole in the golden cube goes out. Candela is left in total darkness, locked up in a cold, dark cell made out of gold and measuring six by six metres. Her heart sinks. She goes around in circles, looking for some kind of help. In the midst of the darkness, she finds it and pauses. A small intermittent light on one of the walls indicates what must be the next step. Could it be a trap? What difference would it make? If Warnes had wanted her to die she'd be dead by now, so why not continue the game for a bit longer? Even though she doesn't want to think about it, Candela cannot stop asking herself what will happen when she reaches the end. If she makes it.

TICK-TOCK TICK-TOCK TICK-TOCK TICK-TOCK

Castian Warnes, the great manipulator. He's all about keeping people down, giving a person confidence and then taking it away until he's destroyed them and made them his prisoner. And this is exactly what the Wanstein Club members are doing with Europe. Manipulating the continent, pounding it down until they provoke mistrust and fear of the markets. Sadly, this is easier to achieve than you think. The key to their success is the investors' belief that 'old Europe' is over. It doesn't matter if it's a lie.

When a government loses the confidence of the people, it only increases the distance between those who view life from above and those who see it from below. But when a government loses the confidence of investors, that government will inevitably be beaten.

Europe is sensitive. Not long ago, its citizens suffered terribly. A crisis lasting several years and corrupt government has hit it where it hurts, where people cannot be trusted. With a bit of help, the markets will reach a turning point. Everything is ready. The Wanstein Club only has to say the word and panic will ensue.

TICK-TOCK TICK-TOCK TICK-TOCK TICK-TOCK

Candela moves her finger above the small light switch; it feels colder and much smoother than the wall. She closes her eyes and presses it. Click. Suddenly, there is light.

She's dazzled by thousands of lights; dots of colour dance about, illuminating her. When she turns, the lights move around her, creating a rainbow that stays close to her. Candela turns, surrounded by a universe of stars. A rush of anxiety. The lights are so beautiful that they make her want to stay here forever. Candela turns around and around and stops. She fixes her gaze on one of the walls, the one in which she can see the silhouette of a door. A black rectangle in the middle of a firmament of stars. She approaches it and grabs the doorknob. A word can be seen in each corner of the room. In each of the letters she can feel the power, darkness and harshness of a voice. A voice that fills the space. The voice of Castian Warnes.

Find me.

It's not a challenge. It's an order.

19

On this page, the puzzle still hasn't been solved.
Find the code to know where to continue.
If you need to, consult the clues on page 161.
Write the code here so you can remember it later on.

CANDELA SOLVES THE LETTER-MAZE PUZZLE

She has 10 minutes left to live.

TICK-TOCK TICK-TOCK TICK-TOCK TICK-TOCK

Left
Forwards
Left
Left
Right
Forwards
Right
Forwards
Right
Left
Forwards
Right
Left

Candela is still lost in the maze and she has less than 10 minutes left.

THE PATH

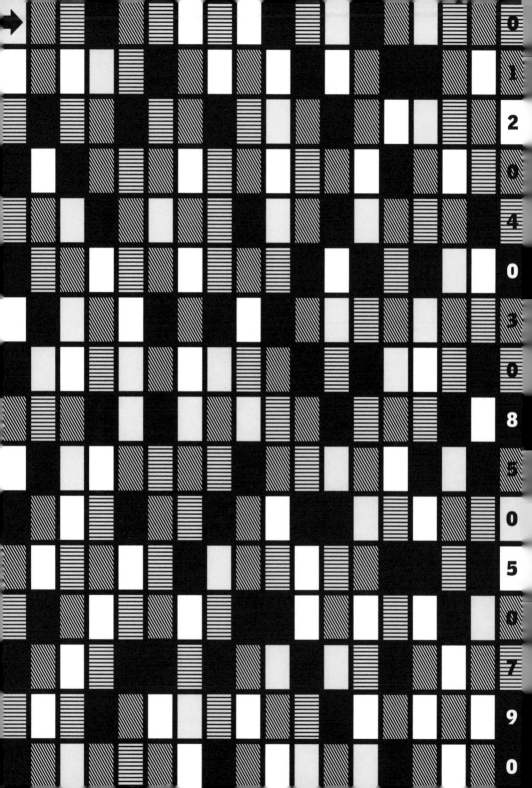

On this page, the puzzle still hasn't been solved.
Find the code to know where to continue.
If you need to, consult the clues on page 165.
Write the code here so you can remember it later on.

CANDELA SOLVES THE TELEPHONE PUZZLE

She runs out of time.

TICK-TOCK TICK-TOCK TICK-TOCK TICK-TOCK

Just as Candela suspects, Warnes is observing her from the other side of the madness. His skin is so close to hers that they could be one person.

He's so close to her; he can see she's on the brink of succumbing to the inevitable. He admires her, because even though she knows she may die, there's not even a trace of defeat in her. It may be due to fatigue, or perhaps it's the pride of a person who knows she has done everything she can. If she dies, she will die fighting until the very end.

Things have moved on very quickly after the telephone call. Warnes notices Candela's determination as she decides which antidote to select. Her breathing, her neck, the look in her eyes. She's like him. A predator.

Ten seconds before the time limit, Candela injects herself with the vaccine and falls into the armchair, exhausted.

Good.

Survival. Warnes cannot remember his own name, just as he cannot remember anyone else's. He has grown accustomed to living with the illness. It does, to a certain extent, have its advantages. He only has to make the effort to remember the names of people who interest him. The rest don't take up any space in his mind. A second to recall the mnemonic, and the name appears.

A face that lights up like a candle… Candela…

Warnes is too clever to allow himself to be arrogant. He did not build the Daedalus for the reasons people think. He did not build it for keeping his secrets or to challenge people.

How absurd. He did it to give those who spend their lives meddling in his affairs something to do.

Give people an impossible challenge and they will kill themselves trying to overcome it. While they are busy trying to overcome it, they will not discover your secret.

As simple as that. Just another trick from the great magician of manipulation.

But Warnes had not expected anyone to break the Daedalus. And he had definitely not expected to be pleased if they did. She was not the first to try, but she is the first to beat it. No one has ever won the respect of Warnes so quickly.

He had known that Candela was preparing for the final assault. He has informers everywhere. But when his phone alerted him to the fact that the intruder had entered the second room, he focused all his attention on her. Warnes rarely gets the opportunity to size himself up against an equal. He had found out everything about her, but had missed the most important thing: she does not jump off moving trains.

Warnes enters the Victorian room through the secret door in the library.

Hello, face that lights up like a candle... Candela.

Her eyes are closed and she's startled, but she smiles inside. She's not mad. She doesn't get up from the armchair, she isn't strong enough. She looks at him. His immaculate suit, his appearance, the scent of expensive cologne, the perfectly cut grey hair. Eyes that smile at her meaningfully, without moving a single facial muscle. Then she looks at her stained blouse and the party skirt, which is ripped to shreds.

'Go to hell,' she thinks. Instead, she asks, 'Did you enjoy the show?'

Very much.

'What now?'

They look directly at each other. Candela, with what remains of her anger; Warnes, with the calm serenity of the man who knows he is in charge. He takes a bottle and two wine glasses from a drinks cabinet.

Now, a glass of wine.

He shows her the bottle of Château Mouton Rothschild.

'I can't have done anything wrong, then,' replies Candela, sarcastically.

In reality, it's about the special vintage, my dear. The only year in the 20th century that the wine did not change, despite being turned 180 degrees. The price is irrelevant. What matters is that it is the best.

He uncorks the bottle and leaves it to breathe. Candela's mind cannot help itself, and she immediately launches into solving the riddle.

'1961.'

Exactly.

Candela knows that while he seems perfectly nice, Warnes is capable of killing her without batting an eyelid. He has no qualms about doing this to her, or to anyone else who stands between him and his objective, whether that is world domination or a simple bottle of wine. She knows they cannot both win and she has already lost too much time.

'Will I get out of here?'

Yes.

'Alive?'

Warnes smiles, tilts his head, then sits next to her on the sofa.

Do you really think that killing you is the worst I could do to you? You are smarter than that, Candela.

She won't take this despicable man at his word. Even if there is no proof, she'll take a risk. What does it matter if he sees her cards?

'I will not let Operation White Bull succeed, Castian. I will not let you ruin Europe.'

Castian decants the wine and fills the two glasses. He hands one to Candela.

None of that matters now, my dear.

Candela has a dry mouth. She takes two large sips of wine, which burn her throat. Water. What she really wants is water.

'What do you mean it doesn't matter? In five days, you and your people are going to wipe out Europe! You're going to condemn two entire generations to poverty. You're going to rob us of our future, for the simple reason that you and your people want to be a little bit richer. And you say that it doesn't matter?'

You're wrong, says Warnes, as he sniffs the wine.

Candela takes another sip; her mouth is dry.

'Am I wrong? What do you think will happen when currencies get destroyed? Come on, Warnes, I'm not an idiot. You have this all sorted out – and well sorted, at that. But I'm not stopping until I've taken you all down. If you want to kill me, do it now.'

Warnes looks at her and reaches into his pocket. Is this how it ends? He takes out a mobile phone and presses a button. The computer screens start working.

Don't be so melodramatic. It won't be in five days.

Candela watches as news programmes from across the world all report the same story. Europe's stock exchanges all show red numbers and continue to free fall. Each time the graph is updated, the line goes lower. They talk about the break-up of the European Union, about the millions of people who have hit the streets in protest, the big companies being attacked by mobs. Candela downs the dregs of her wine in a single mouthful. Her senses are becoming more heightened by the moment. Her eyes linger on the date visible on the bottom-right screen. She looks at Warnes, questioningly.

You've not been asleep for minutes, like I've led you to believe. It's been two weeks, my dear. If I had not left you out of the game all of this time, I would have had no choice but to kill you. Operation White Bull cannot be delayed. It is not my fault that the governments do not act as they should. You already know that all I do is buy and sell.

Candela cries. She has come down to this living hell to fight the monster and her heart has been burned forever. Warnes has won. He had already won before the game had begun. Candela puts down the wine glass on the table. It falls over. Suddenly, she tries to hurl herself at Warnes – she wants to kill him. But her body does not react. Warnes does not move. He looks at her, raises his glass as if to make a toast, then places it on top of the marble table. Now Candela understands.

'You bastard!'

Do not be scared. Tomorrow, you will wake up in your bed and you will not remember anything.

He gets up and heads for the door by which he had entered. As she watches him leave Candela makes a decision. She knows it's almost impossible. That it's a matter of seconds, the time it'll take her to go from the door to the place Warnes will emerge from. Then to the hidden chamber that must lie a few metres from there, where he sits and observes her. She gathers all her strength and gets ready. As he leaves the room, Warnes turns and nods, as if to dismiss her. Candela must try, she cannot give up yet. Not when the wheels have started turning.

The screens flicker between news and graphs, but one of them remains black. If she can access the computer, maybe everything that she has overcome so far will have been worth it. The door closes. Without losing a second, she approaches the table of computers, her every movement making her contract with pain. The screen is not switched off. When she looks at it closely, a strange alphabet of letters and numbers can be made out in the darkness. In the middle, the final puzzle.

CODE.

Playtime is over.

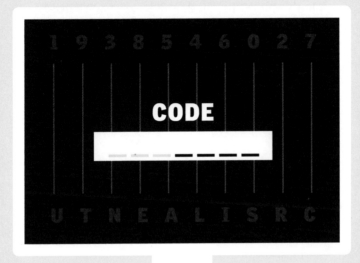

35

On this page, the puzzle still hasn't been solved.
Find the code to know where to continue.
If you need to, consult the clues on page 175.
Write the code here so you can remember it later on.

CANDELA SOLVES THE METAL-PLATE PUZZLE

She has 50 minutes left to live.

TICK-TOCK TICK-TOCK TICK-TOCK TICK-TOCK

Candela inserts the code that she had found in the metal-plate puzzle and carefully turns the handle. She has 50 minutes left. She has a look of concentration, her breathing is controlled, her muscles ready for combat. The door opens. Candela pushes it and waits. The door reaches its limit and Candela releases her breath, which she had been holding in. She is tired, very tired. But she has no alternative but to continue. She shouts into the darkness that unfurls in front of her.

'My name is Candela Fuertes – and I am going to escape!'

TICK-TOCK TICK-TOCK TICK-TOCK TICK-TOCK

Castian Warnes. The big man. The man who's been in her mind ever since she began investigating him. As hard as she tries to get him out of her head, she fails. Fifty-two years old, grey temples, an abundance of hair, grey eyes, square fingernails. Smart, understated and dangerous. From what she has gathered from her research, Warnes had a difficult childhood. Born in Albania, he was orphaned when he was 11. He survived and moved away, first to France, then to the United States, where he studied economics. He did so, like many others before him, but there was one difference: he is now outrageously rich.

The investigation into Warnes had begun almost fortuitously several months earlier, as part of a routine job. On revising the papers of a law firm that had been passed to the newspaper by a source, Candela got a major shock.

Companies, companies, companies. Candela discovered that

Warnes was setting up new companies or buying old ones of no apparent value. None of them were in Europe; the vast majority were in tax havens like the Bahamas, Panama or the Philippines. This in itself was not a crime, but it was enough to make Candela want to continue her investigation. The number of organisations being opened by Warnes was incredible, totally lacking in logic. It goes without saying that these companies were not in his name: they were presided over by minor owners, frontmen or family members. But the wolf was always there at the end of the chain. And not just him: there was a whole pack, lying in wait. Other magnates like him were doing the same thing. The four, led by Warnes, who made up the Wanstein Club were flooding the world with their ghost companies.

At five in the morning Candela tapped a number into her phone. 'Boss, we have a story.'

She put on her leggings and running shoes and went out into the street. In her mind, there was one image and one target: Castian Warnes, owner of one of the biggest investment groups in the world and self-appointed King Midas of the world of finance.

In her final year at university, Candela had shared a flat with Mark, a computer addict. They were friends with benefits. Over the course of living with him, Candela had learnt a bit about sex and a lot about the stock exchange.

Whenever she got home from a night on the town in the early hours, she would find him engrossed in front of the computer. He'd be sitting there with a cup of coffee in his hand and all five senses focused on the screen.

'Mark, are you coming?'

'Straight away, Candela. Hang on a minute, the Hong Kong stock exchange is about to open...'

Or London, or New York. Whichever one. There was always a trading floor just about to open. Even though Mark's voice said, 'I'm on my way', his body said 'not today'.

Tired, and asking herself why she was still with this idiot, Candela sat down on the sofa and waited for him. She grabbed a blanket and asked him questions about the stock exchange.

'Is it going up or down today?'

'Down, Candela, down. Let's chat later.'

Shut in the second of the Daedalus rooms, Candela remembered Mark's words as he explained that you could make lots of money at the expense of others.

'When it goes down? But you make money if you buy shares and they go up, don't you? How can you make money if they go down?'

'You can bet that something in the stock exchange will go down. For example, you could bet that a company will go bust or that a company will not repay its debt.'

'But that's awful!'

'Why?'

'Because you are betting that things will go badly for people.'

'I don't do that. I only buy and sell stocks.'

'Are you joking?'

Mark was the one who taught her the basics about the stock exchange. In the beginning, she listened more out of flirtatiousness than interest. Soon, the new fatigue of her so-called boyfriend was inversely proportional to his interest in the finance world – the people pulling the strings in the darkness, the ones who very few people actually knew.

'Candela, these people are gods! George Soros! Oh my God, this man made a billion dollars in just one day!'

'Who?' Soros, the one Mark referred to as 'god', had caused the fall of the pound sterling in 1992.

Luckily, after all that, it would have been difficult for any more of this sort of thing to happen. Current regulations and limitations prevent it, but nothing is impossible in the stock exchange if you have enough money.

Thinking about it in an abstract way, the enormity of what Soros had achieved would have been worthy of admiration – if it hadn't been for one thing. Candela could not ignore the fact that this money had effectively been paid out by the most disadvantaged people.

Candela knows that Warnes is a wealth scavenger – and one of the worst of them. That is why she decided to follow him, watching and waiting patiently for the day to come when he made a single mistake, a single illegality so that he would be framed. The day came.

Initially she could not believe that Warnes would try to do something similar to what Soros had done. Then she discovered that what he was going to do was, in fact, much worse.

'I swore I'd expose people like you, Warnes.'

TICK-TOCK TICK-TOCK TICK-TOCK TICK-TOCK

Now, shut in the maze she had entered herself, she counts the minutes. Only 49 left. Absorbed by her own thoughts, Candela hasn't made any further progress, and now looks around the new space opening up before her. She goes through the door and it closes behind her. Warnes is not going to make it easy.

'I swore that I would pursue people like you.'

Candela observes, touches, smells. She knows that speed is vital if she is to survive. She has to proceed quickly, but without running. The new space is identical to the previous one: six by six metres, grey walls, a plate of light. A dry metallic smell overwhelms everything. Is it the room? The poison? She can't allow her brain to be submerged in fear. Onwards, always onwards. Step by step, one hand, then the other.

She makes out three concealed mirrors on the wall to her left. She approaches one of them carefully. She does not trust Warnes' Machiavellian mind. She fixes her gaze on the central mirror and imagines him on the other side, watching her.

41

'Do you like what you see?'

Lines have been drawn on two of the mirrors. One of them has a vertical line; the other has an inverted C. She can also see something reflected in the mirrors. There are three numbers: 1, 3 and 5.

'Come on, Candela – don't rush this, but don't stop.'

There's a numerical keypad on the door that she should presumably use to get out of the space. Even though she knows it couldn't be so easy, Candela approaches and types in the numbers she found on the wall. Beep. Just as she thought, it doesn't work. But she already knows that the combination consists of three numbers. 'I could do with one of your coffees right now, Mark.'

Candela crouches down. Her eyes are heavy. She squints, then rests her eyes for a moment before breathing. She starts again. Three mirrors, some lines and three numbers. An entire world depends on these three pieces of evidence.

She has 47 minutes left.

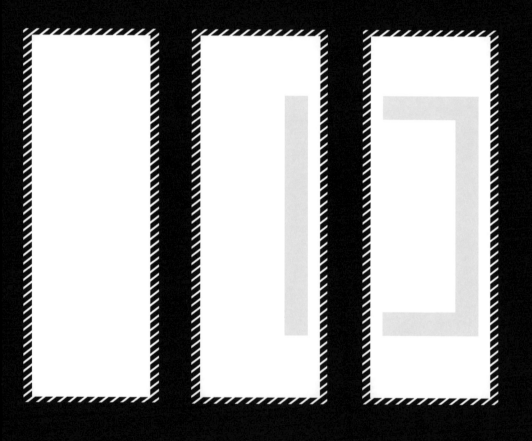

On this page, the puzzle still hasn't been solved.
Find the code to know where to continue.
If you need to, consult the clues on page 145.
Write the code here so you can remember it later on.

CANDELA SOLVES THE METAL-BARRED-GATE PUZZLE

She has 36 minutes left to live.

TICK-TOCK TICK-TOCK TICK-TOCK TICK-TOCK

Candela moves the handle into the correct position and the metal-barred gate opens. As soon as she has passed through the gap, the gate moves back into place behind her. She stops. A second or two, no more. Enough time to relax her mind and to distance herself. She only has 36 minutes. He saw her enter the castle, she's sure of it. Is he letting her in, even though he knows what she's looking for? Trapped in a maze, Candela asks herself why she always has to stick her nose into things that don't matter.

'That's a lie. This does matter to me. Of course it matters to me.'

She continues through the tunnel, beneath the intermittent light, walking towards the unknown.

TICK-TOCK TICK-TOCK TICK-TOCK TICK-TOCK

Candela had intensified her research when she had seen what the Wanstein Club was planning amid the web of faces, threads and drawing pins she had created. She first became aware of her worst nightmare when she was following the trail of declassified emails in a money-laundering trial. On looking at it alongside information from her Trojans, she came across Operation White Bull.

Candela had finished an article on the Greek debt crisis just before beginning her investigation into the Warnes case. Had it not been for this, she may not have noticed it. According to Greek mythology, Zeus took the form of a white bull when he kidnapped and dishonoured the goddess Europa. Was it a coincidence? All of

Candela's instincts were activated. She followed the thread and was astonished by what she discovered. It had catastrophic implications.

As Candela had suspected, this time the Wanstein Club would not settle for making thousands of euros simulating a rise in the markets. The ambitions of the club knew no limits. They wanted more. They wanted to ruin Europe and destroy the euro! Candela couldn't imagine the suffering that this would cause to millions of normal people like herself. This is what Warnes and his club of rich people wanted to do, to screw up Europe!

It was not enough to emulate George Soros. They wanted to do more. He had destroyed a country – they would destroy Europe. Could they actually do it? You need a lot of money to destroy a currency. Soros had done it with derivatives, which were now more closely regulated. But five of the most powerful men in the world, with the help of Chinese capital? Of course they could.

Candela had spent the past couple of months getting under the skin of Castian Warnes, thinking with his brain, feeling his selfishness, sleeping through his dreams, breathing his morning breath. But even though she knew what she was looking for, she couldn't find anything. She had no proof, only powerlessness.

'Boss, the Wanstein Club wants to destroy Europe. They're making a colossal number of pointless investments from businesses dotted all over the world.'

'Where's the proof? I need proof!'

Candela had run out of leads. The Daedalus – the place where Warnes kept his secrets – was the only thing left. Her intuition was telling her that this was where she would find all the proof she could want. This was why, when she discovered that the Wanstein Club was organising its annual charity ball (in aid of childhood poverty) in Ferulic Castle, the mansion owned by Warnes, she asked her boss to get her an invitation.

'But Candela, what if only the glossy magazines are going?'

'Then make something up. Work your contacts, sleep with whoever, do whatever you like. But I have to get in.' 'And are you going to wear a long dress?' she asked, as she hid her joking eyes behind the last set of photos that Candela had left on her desk.

'A long dress and red lipstick, if needs be.'

All her leads had dried up. She needed air. Candela was stubborn and pig-headed. On several occasions, it had cost her dearly; on others, it had allowed her to gain a reputation for being a rock-solid journalist.

TICK-TOCK TICK-TOCK TICK-TOCK TICK-TOCK

Silence. Candela looks ahead. She observes, smells, listens. She moves.

Music starts to enter her ears, distantly at the start, then getting louder as she moves forward. It's *The Blue Danube* by Strauss. Candela stops suddenly. This waltz is the one she used to dance with her father when she was a girl.

'How much do you know about me, Warnes?'

Long-forgotten memories come flooding back. Her little feet on her father's, her small hands holding his strong fingers tightly.

'Father...'

Warnes knew Candela would go to Ferulic Castle. He was waiting for her. He knew what she wanted and he let her enter. For him, it was only a game; for her it was not. It was about the destruction of millions of jobs, millions condemned to misery, parents who would not know how to feed their children. And even though Candela's vocation wasn't to be a hero, she knew that if she let this happen without even trying to stop it, she'd never be able to look at herself again. That is how she came to be here, locked in a maze wearing bright red lipstick, 34 minutes away from death.

Candela loves her job. She lives it with an intensity that others can only dream of, forever on the verge of unveiling the truth at all costs, though it may end her life. And it isn't because Candela is brave, even though she'd promised herself she wouldn't just lie down whenever problems came along, like her father used to. Although that was a perfectly respectable decision, it was not for her. She promised herself that she would always carry on until the end, however hard that might be.

One-two-three, one-two-three, one-two-three, one-two-three...

On hearing those bars of *The Blue Danube*, her pulse quickened again.

'Dad...'

The Blue Danube ends.

'At last.'

The Blue Danube starts up again. It's on a loop. With Castian Warnes, nothing happens by chance, and Candela knows it. Vulnerability. That's what he's looking for. Her vulnerability. But she won't give it to him, at least not for now. She starts to hum along, in time with the music.

One-two-three, one-two-three, one-two-three, one-two-three...

On entering the Daedalus, Candela knew what she would find. Riddles and more riddles. Now, listening to the notes of *The Blue Danube*, she isn't sure whether she had discovered this labyrinth by chance or whether he had wanted her to discover it.

Warnes suffers a strain of dysmnesia called onomagnosia. He can't remember names, numbers or years. Warnes is incapable of remembering his telephone number, his computer password or his butler's name straight away. He creates ways – mnemonics, clues and logic problems – to help him reach his objective without aiming straight for it. Hence the security system.

The Daedalus is a big achievement.

If there's one person who can get out of the world's best escape room, it's Candela.

'Your greatest achievement, your greatest source of pride, your greatest weakness.'

Although Candela doesn't want to think about it, she knows she feels darkly attracted to Warnes, towards the centre of the maze. She throws herself into her investigations. When researching someone, she thinks like them and feels like them. She is them.

She moves through the tunnel with the waltz playing in the background, remembering her father, dancing with her father.

'Candela, when you look at a dance from far away, it is something fluid, sublime and magnificent. But if you get closer and look carefully, you will see that a dance is made up of one step after another. You can arrive wherever you want to arrive, if you go one step at a time.'

'What does *sublime* mean?' asked the little girl.

Step, step, light, step, step, light. The music is getting louder. Candela moves forwards under the tunnel lights. Darkness. Light. Darkness. Travelling across the concrete walls, which feel so sterile.

She knew that the Daedalus had a gruesome security system. She knew she'd die if she did not find the antidote. But she couldn't give up, especially not at this stage. She must continue. She must find the clues, she must find the antidote, she must find the exit. If she doesn't succeed, the group will win and the losers will lose everything. Warnes is a player. He has a sickening passion for riddles and has his own version of Ariadne's thread. The man is addicted to gambling on the suffering of others, but he'll never turn down a good opponent. This is how Candela knows that she is capable of taking him on.

The light switches on and off above her head. Even so, Candela can see something on the floor. It goes away, then comes back. Darkness. Light. She watches. It recedes. It moves back to one side. Then she sees them. There are prints. They look like partial footprints in the middle of a film of dust. Candela crouches down and touches them. They are carved out of the cement floor.

She tiptoes forwards, taking mental images of the footprints she comes across. She cannot go back, there's not a moment to lose. At the end of the tunnel she will find another door, she knows it. Another keypad, she knows that too. And she will be ready.

When her hands find the end of the tunnel, Candela gazes at the door ahead of her.

Deep in the bowels of Ferulic Castle, a young woman with a mane of auburn hair and almost translucent skin is closing her eyes. She visualises the footprints she had mentally recorded only moments ago. She then reads aloud the phrase that has been engraved on the door.

'The emphasis is the code.'

Just metres away, members of the Wanstein Club – the world's real government – make themselves feel good by celebrating what they claim is a gala benefit. Tycoons cleaning up their act. They will undoubtedly also be dancing a waltz.

One-two-three, one-two-three, one-two-three, one-two-three…

'I'm coming, Warnes. I'm coming.'

She looks at the stopwatch. 32 minutes.

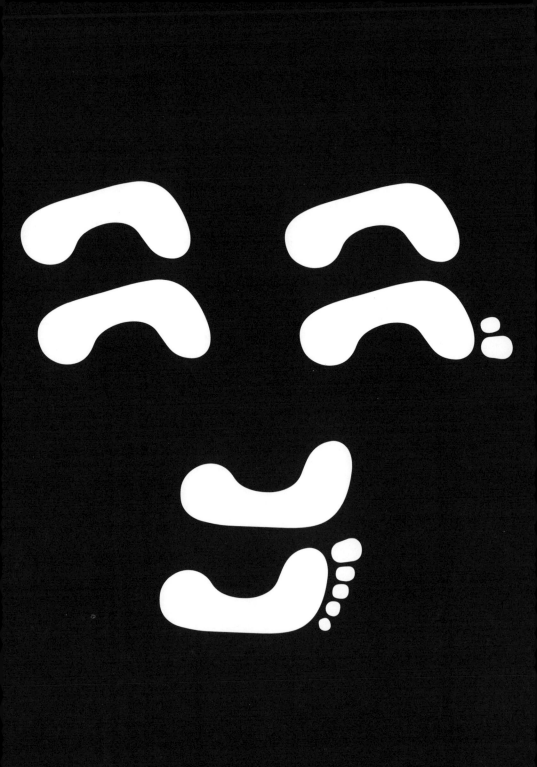

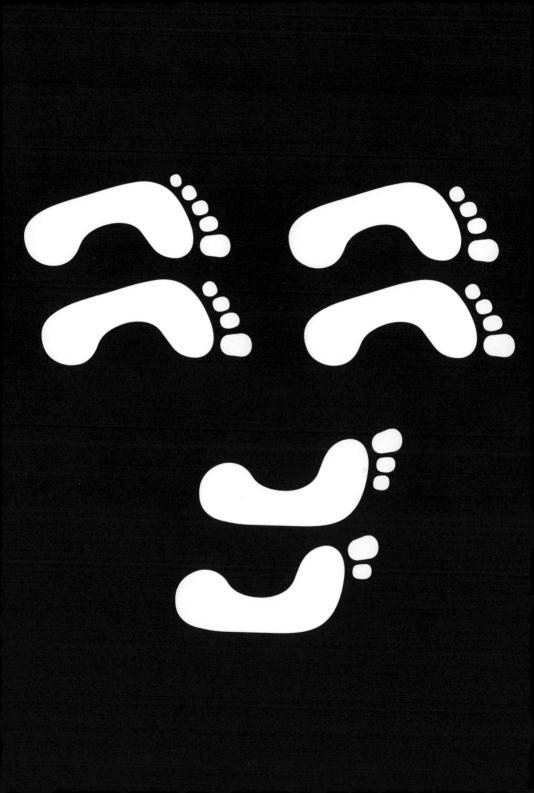

On this page, the puzzle still hasn't been solved.
Find the code to know where to continue.
If you need to, consult the clues on page 149.
Write the code here so you can remember it later on.

CANDELA SOLVES THE COMPUTER PUZZLE

This is the end.

When she opens her eyes, she sees that the time on her alarm clock is 9am. The sun is still weak, making the room gloomy. Candela gets up and sees that her party skirt and white blouse are lying tidily on the chair next to the bed. She lies there looking at them. She can't remember getting home or undressing. She's surprised to see that her clothes are so neatly folded. She has always had a rather unconventional view of what it means to be tidy. She massages her temples. Her head hurts.

'What a blur.'

Her memories from the night before are hazy. She knows that she was at the charity gala in aid of fighting childhood poverty. It had been organised by Castian Warnes and his little friends in the Wanstein Club. She remembers entering Ferulic Castle and being surprised by the sobriety and elegance. While the internationally wealthy arrived in their luxury cars, she and the rest of the press had stayed in a corner of the garden. Then, Warnes had appeared in person at the top of the staircase. Her heart had skipped a beat. Close up, Warnes exuded a certain magnetism that was difficult to describe. As the King Midas of finance entered the castle, patting the latest arrival on the back with one hand, he turned around and signalled to the journalists that they could now enter the room set aside for them. Candela got the impression that his eyes lingered on her for a second longer than necessary.

She feels cold, so she puts on her old navy-blue cardigan over her pyjamas and leaves the room. On opening the door, she's greeted by photos, news and newspaper cuttings of Warnes, staring down at her from each of the walls. Candela makes a cup of coffee and sits down on the futon, which also serves as a sofa. Looking at her surroundings, she tries to remember what happened last night. She knows she didn't manage to get into the infamous Daedalus, Warnes' supposed safety deposit box. That had been her objective, her reason for being there. The last thing she can remember is that she'd flirted with a correspondent from one of the country's financial newspapers, and that she'd done so with a glass of whisky in her hand. That in itself is strange, because she usually prefers beer to spirits.

'You had a chance and you blew it.'

She had never experienced anything like this in all of her life as a reporter. She is a professional who never mixes work with pleasure.

Annoyed with herself, she goes to take a shower. When she gets undressed, she realises that she has broken some of her nails. Her entire body hurts. Her arms and legs are covered in bruises and she has no memory of how they got there. She turns on the shower and stands under the stream of cold water. The drops of water pierce her like needles and she squeals in pain. But it might help her to think.

When she gets out of the shower, she's still shivering, even in her bathrobe. She makes herself another cup of coffee and sits down in front of the computer. She turns it on and goes to get dressed. She leaves her bedroom door open while she dresses in jeans and a black woollen jumper that is two sizes too big. As she dresses, she looks at a picture of Warnes that she has stuck on the wall. Candela curses herself for getting so carried away, but not actually managing to get hold of a single piece of proof of what the Wanstein Club are hoping to achieve.

She clicks on the email icon. A little brown envelope informs her that she has 11 new messages. She opens the inbox and looks at the names of the senders, starting with the oldest email.

'What?'

Candela sent herself an email scarcely six hours ago. Surprised, she opens it. The message is empty, even though it has an attachment. She double-clicks on the icon and waits for the document to download. She looks at the date.

'What?'

Crash!

The coffee cup falls on the floor and breaks into a thousand little pieces. She cannot believe her eyes. She saves the document on a USB stick, grabs her leather jacket and runs out of the door. She goes down the stairs two at a time, running as fast as she can. When she goes past the rubbish bin two blocks from her house, out of the corner of her eye she sees that there is a bundle of clothes in it. It is her dirty crumpled blouse and her ripped party skirt. She turns and looks up at the window of her house, down the street. Her entire body shudders.

Two years have passed. The collapse of the euro has taken many futures with it. Europe is not the same anymore.

Today is the first day of the Wanstein Club trial.

It is only a matter of time.

From: Castian Warnes
Subject: Do you really think it's all over?

cocolisto.com/escapebook/eng/mail

CANDELA SOLVES THE
NUMBER-MAZE PUZZLE

She has 7 minutes left to live.

TICK-TOCK TICK-TOCK TICK-TOCK TICK-TOCK

Candela can't concentrate. Her legs are becoming weaker and her mouth is very dry. She needs water. She can now hardly feel her right hand. She leans one of her shoulders against the wall. She doesn't know how long she has been walking around, lost. She thinks that it has been a long time, even though, when she looks at the stopwatch, it says that a lot less time has passed. She's scared. She closes her eyes, but she cannot sleep. She's sure that if she does, she won't wake up.

She loses her balance. For a moment, her right hand comes away from the wall, then, with a whimper, it returns. She must not become disoriented. There is no time to lose. Candela looks for images that will help to keep her awake. She remembers the beaches she used to visit with her father every summer. She learnt to swim there. When she used to get into the water, it felt like a rebirth. Afterwards, the sun would burn her back while she made sandcastles.

The darkness returns.

She isn't managing to focus on pleasant images. She remembers. Warnes, the Wanstein Club, Operation White Bull. In five days, they will sell millions of euros. Once they have achieved their objective, they will knock down the castle called Europe, burying it beneath the sand and a sea of waste that will flood everything.

Candela leans her back against the wall, heaves, slips and falls to the floor. But before sitting down, before stopping, before the fear of faltering, she makes an effort and gets on all fours. She continues to crawl along like this, like a wounded animal. She touches the wall with the back of her right hand, using the rest of her body to focus all her remaining effort: first on one leg and then on the other. Muscle, knee, calf, muscle, knee, calf. Candela moves forwards like this, keeping her eyes focused on the floor, feeling the cold wall the whole time. She's trying to win the race of life, the race for a life that is slipping away with every breath she takes.

'Did you want to see me on my knees? Here I am. You've got me where you want me. But don't misunderstand, this is not surrender.'

Is that what she's saying? Is that what she thinks? Her mind is getting weaker and weaker. She is becoming more and more confused. Ouch! Something is stuck to her knee. She moves backwards, without letting go of the wall, and sees something engraved on the floor. She traces it with her free hand. Suddenly, her senses come alive.

Is this the end? A new test? She contains herself. This is precisely what she should not do, to lose discipline. When you are in a maze, you have to be methodical until the end. If you make an error, you have to go back to the start – and right now, there is no time for that. There are 7 minutes left. Candela keeps crawling, staying alert for signals. She keeps her eyes focused on the piece of floor ahead of her.

Muscle, knee, calf. Another engraving. Muscle, knee, calf. Another engraving. Hand by hand, step by step... 'A door!'

Candela allows herself a moment's rest. She lies down with her mouth open to get her strength back. A laugh – or is it a sigh of relief? – comes from her exhausted lungs.

Lying on the floor with her legs stretched out and her face against the cold stone, Candela opens her eyes and sees it. Everything depends on the viewing angle.

'Gotcha!'

⏃	▽	△	⏀
9	1	6	2
⏃	▽	△	⏀
7	9	3	0
⏃	▽	△	⏀
5	2	0	8

On this page, the puzzle still hasn't been solved.
Find the code to know where to continue.
If you need to, consult the clues on page 169.
Write the code here so you can remember it later on.

CANDELA SOLVES THE LIGHT-ROOM PUZZLE

She has 12 minutes left to live.

TICK-TOCK TICK-TOCK TICK-TOCK TICK-TOCK

When Candela puts the key in the lock, the world trembles. The earth moves and she huddles up on the floor. On the other side of the cube walls, there is a big crashing sound. She doesn't know what is happening. Beneath her, everything is vibrating. The sound is thunderous. Candela covers her ears, and huddles up even more. Suddenly, silence.

The black door between the thousands of lights opens. A long, illuminated corridor appears before her. Candela gets up and goes towards the light. Where before there had been a huge room, now there are walls and pathways with forks in them. She begins walking. One step, another step then another. Right? Left? One step, another step. Right? Left?

'A maze. A maze within a maze!'

She needs air. She does not know how many puzzles lie between her and the antidote, she doesn't know whether the Candela who has spent 44 minutes moving around the Daedalus will reach the end.

'How much further, Warnes?'

Silence. Although Warnes' last words still reverberate in her head.

Find me.

Candela looks in front of her. All she can do is carry on. She puts her right hand on one of the cold walls of the maze and walks. If the maze is not concentric, sooner or later she should get out of here. All she has to do is put her hand on the wall and keep in contact with it. If she reaches the edge, she will eventually find the exit. One step, another step. Now everything depends on the distance that she has to cover.

TICK-TOCK TICK-TOCK TICK-TOCK TICK-TOCK

As she progresses through the maze, she remembers the first time she had become interested in the word 'economy'. As one of her teachers used to say, it is a beautiful word when balanced.

'Economy is the science that studies how to organise society, so as to produce its means of existence and then distribute it between its members. It is the economy that allows society to create more of a product once it has been consumed. In doing so, it can therefore supply society with that base material as a whole in a constant and sustainable way.'

A nice definition for a word that directly affects people's lives. Candela thinks about the little that those people generally know about the word. The real economy moves in uncertain waves, rather than in certain constancy. Euphoria and panic. Like a river. If the current is strong, it is difficult to dominate. But when it calms, everyone is prepared to wade and bathe in it, and to build dams that guide the water.

TICK-TOCK TICK-TOCK TICK-TOCK TICK-TOCK

Candela has stopped without realising it. Her feet are not moving. Everything is confusing. Bang. She hits the wall with her hands. Bang. With her legs. Bang. With her entire body. Pain. And the adrenaline returns to get her up and moving again.

'A maze. You have put me in another bloody maze.'

Step by step, Candela nears the end, whatever it may be. She has less than 11 minutes left.

P	F	A	D	A	L	S	M	R	T	A	C	F	O
W	O	R	D	R	O	D	R	R	N	D	O	M	P
Z	L	A	T	E	G	O	C	U	R	S	N	H	R
X	L	T	N	D	R	I	L	D	E	J	T	E	O
Y	O	I	S	T	O	R	I	A	P	K	R	C	D
N	W	T	H	E	I	T	Y	O	R	T	U	U	A
A	D	C	W	P	M	L	M	P	L	Y	B	R	R
K	M	A	P	A	R	T	Z	W	K	O	C	E	O
N	O	M	M	T	E	J	N	A	B	V	O	D	B
J	A	I	P	H	L	I	F	O	A	S	I	T	A
Q	B	D	N	A	R	Z	U	W	Z	H	X	A	L
Z	P	Y	Y	T	M	B	T	S	W	I	A	W	O
V	U	O	D	I	S	C	Y	S	T	R	E	S	C
T	R	U	E	G	J	L	M	O	T	X	D	P	Y
W	L	W	I	L	L	E	A	D	W	D	O	M	P
Z	C	I	C	R	F	E	R	O	Z	Z	N	H	R
X	U	D	U	E	I	E	K	P	X	E	T	E	O
Y	H	E	B	D	N	E	U	A	Y	E	R	C	D
N	L	N	R	T	D	V	I	O	N	R	I	U	A
A	D	R	E	H	T	A	P	R	A	H	B	R	R
K	M	Z	C	U	E	L	N	U	K	T	X	E	O
N	O	Y	O	V	A	C	V	T	W	O	M	D	B
J	A	L	D	A	Z	E	R	O	J	J	E	T	A
Q	B	B	E	I	S	J	A	L	Q	Q	S	A	L
Z	P	A	D	R	G	Q	X	E	Z	Z	A	W	O
V	U	X	O	G	S	Z	M	N	V	V	N	Q	C

On this page, the puzzle still hasn't been solved.
Find the code to know where to continue.
If you need to, consult the clues on page 163.
Write the code here so you can remember it later on.

CANDELA SOLVES THE COLOUR-MAZE PUZZLE

She has 8 minutes left to live.

TICK-TOCK TICK-TOCK TICK-TOCK TICK-TOCK

Run. Candela tries to go as fast as she can, but her steps are erratic. At first, the coolness of the wall and the built-up adrenaline had helped her to get her act together. But after every high comes a low.

The same cold that had previously invigorated her now causes her to lose all feeling in her fingers, and the cold spreads to her bones. Drops of sweat are slipping down her forehead, but her body is shaking. She turns to the right. She doesn't know how many endless corridors she has been along. She turns left. Nor does she know the size of the maze inside which she is trapped. She turns left. She can't even be sure there is an exit, nor whether the method she learnt as a child, of keeping her right hand in contact with the wall, will even work. She turns left.

The endless walls still appear all around. The Daedalus, the security system created by a man incapable of remembering names or passwords, is about to finish Candela off.

TICK-TOCK TICK-TOCK TICK-TOCK TICK-TOCK

When Candela discovered the Daedalus existed, there was something that puzzled her. Was Warnes really suffering from a strange mental illness, or was everything a strategy so his rivals lowered their guard?

Warnes never evades questions about his illness when asked, which Candela thinks is strange.

How can a person so guarded about his personal life be so open about something that could be interpreted as a weakness? It doesn't add up. She knows perfectly well that people tend to underestimate those who suffer from unusual conditions. When it became apparent that her father had contracted motor neurone disease, certain people had started speaking loudly and slowly at him, as if he could no longer understand them. Unfortunately, he was completely lucid. Too lucid.

Candela searched and questioned. She even ended up accepting a dinner invitation from a friend's colleague, a man who she really did not like, but who was the neurologist of the moment. 'The fat cats' neurologist', as he put it, while smiling his excessively white smile.

One look down, a couple of drinks and she got it. Candela knew that Warnes had another condition, other than onomagnosia. Hypermnesia, the capacity to remember in sparkling detail things that others forget.

'A super-memory of a precise moment. Can you imagine what it is like to remember everything about a person by looking at them only once?' asked the neurologist, looking Candela up and down with his lecherous eyes.

There was no doubt about it. Warnes was a ticking time bomb for his opponents. At first glance, you'd have thought that when he was having a quiet moment, it was because he was doubtful, insecure or afraid. In actual fact, these silences acted like a smokescreen. He saw you once, and even though he didn't remember your face, he never forgot your scent, the way you move, or the way you are. And not just that. The number of details grew in his mind at the same rate as they would be forgotten by a normal brain. It didn't matter if he couldn't remember your name or the date of your first meeting. He didn't need to know that. The important things stayed in his mind. Forever.

Can anyone really compete with someone like that?

TICK-TOCK TICK-TOCK TICK-TOCK TICK-TOCK

Time is running out. Less than 8 minutes until the end and Candela still hasn't found the way out.

DEECORP OT WOH WONK LLIW UOY
OG UOY SA SPETS EHT PU DDA UOY FI
DNA LANOGAID A NI REVEN
ENIL THGIARTS A NI SYAWLA

CIGOL EHT DNIF

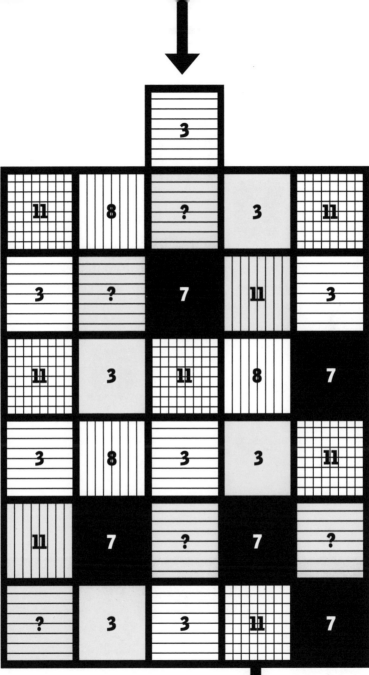

On this page, the puzzle still hasn't been solved.
Find the code to know where to continue.
If you need to, consult the clues on page 167.
Write the code here so you can remember it later on.

CANDELA SOLVES
THE MIRROR PUZZLE

She has 44 minutes left to live.

TICK-TOCK TICK-TOCK TICK-TOCK TICK-TOCK

Candela inserts the code she found in the mirrors. The door opens in front of her, and a tunnel awaits. She can smell the darkness. She can feel the darkness. For her, the Daedalus is a dress that has to be taken out little by little. Will Warnes have made it fit perfectly?

She has 44 minutes left.

She takes off her shoes and walks barefoot, crossing to the other side. The door shuts behind her. Night again.

She inhales deeply, taking in the darkness. Blood and steel. In her veins, she can feel the gas that has entered through her lungs. She doesn't know how it will kill her, whether hers will be a sudden death or a slow one. All she knows is that it will not be pleasant, that's for sure.

'Calm down, Candela. Here and now, think about the here and now.'

There's only one thing she can do: take action and keep moving forwards step by step. Candela musters all her courage and heads into the lion's den that awaits.

Light.

One step in, a dim light goes on above her ahead, illuminating an area of half a metre in diameter around her. Quietly and expectantly, Candela looks at her immediate surroundings. It is the same anodyne grey as before, but more cramped.

She moves forwards.

The light goes out and another light comes on. Step by step, light after light, Candela moves along what seems to be a tunnel with no apparent end. She has 42 minutes left.

TICK-TOCK TICK-TOCK TICK-TOCK TICK-TOCK

Each day, Candela would stay up until the early hours of the morning, trying to get to the bottom of Castian Warnes and the Wanstein Club. It was all dark, dense and unintelligible. However, thread by thread Candela was unravelling the tangle. All her concentration was required to make a mental map of the different financial groups and businesses managed by him.

'I can smell you, Warnes.'

This is what Candela Fuertes does best, what her boss and colleagues admire most about her. Her capacity to get underneath the skin of the nastiest pieces of work in the world, and to discover their deepest, darkest secrets. But it comes at a price. She can't understand anyone without coming to feel something for them. Anger. Admiration. Hate.

Candela had created a file on each of the companies linked to Warnes or the Wanstein Club. In an attempt to cast some light on the situation, she had covered the walls of her living room with notes arranged in chronological order, cuttings, photos and gossip pieces. At night, the images would dance around her head. In the morning, she would rearrange them once again. This all went on with a coffee in one hand and a piece of thread and a handful of red drawing pins in the other. Warnes' face was in the middle of this maze, showing her a different angle on a daily basis.

Darkness.

Light.

She used the drawing pins to mark the location of each new Wanstein company. The red thread joined them together, creating a map that covered some continents and avoided others. Then she saw it: China. The companies formed a spider's web around Europe. The Wanstein Club was buying an extraordinary amount of euros thanks to its links to Chinese tycoons. To achieve their objective, Warnes and his partners needed much more capital than they had at their disposal. Thanks to its network of companies and volume of Chinese capital, the Wanstein Club had created the illusion that the stock market would not stop growing. They shouted it from the rooftops: 'Europe is in recovery!' A straightforward and clear message that newspapers would repeat like a mantra several days later. 'The anticipated economic recovery of the eurozone.' It was an illusion. The markets had swallowed the bait and the investors followed suit. The euro then abandoned the dollar. It was at that moment that Candela had started to realise what the Wanstein Club wanted to achieve. And she was horrified.

TICK-TOCK TICK-TOCK TICK-TOCK TICK-TOCK

The light at the end of the tunnel goes on and off, in a rhythm. With every step, Candela stops, watching where she's going and looking around her, then continuing to move forwards. Too slow. Darkness. Light. In a systematic manner, Candela analyses the walls within reach of the circle of light around her. Nothing. She speeds up as much as she can. Her head is spinning. One step forwards. Pause. Another step. Pause. A footstep. Pause.
Darkness
Light.
Clunk.
Candela bumps into a metal-barred gate. She stops and rubs the side of her face that had hit it. Could she hear laughter? No, just the metallic grating noise of the bars.
An illusion.

TICK-TOCK TICK-TOCK TICK-TOCK TICK-TOCK

The stock market wasn't the only thing Mark had taught her about. He had taught her how to analyse information, as well as how to find patterns and common denominators. Now, Candela is a specialist in all of these things. Even though she knows it is illegal, sometimes in rare instances, when there is no other way, and she thinks that the end justifies the means, she uses Trojans – little pieces of code that glean information from remote computers.

'The things that I've learnt from you, Mark!'

This was how she knew that the Wanstein Club was creating a work of fiction and using the tools most frequently used by vermin the world over: lies.

Take, for example, what happened in the 2008 crash. Numerous mortgages, that would have been difficult to repay, ended up being passed through the shredder by certain banks. They fractioned, hid, concealed and packaged impaired assets in smaller assets, as if they were sweets. The quality agencies happily gobbled them up. 'No danger,' or so they said. 'They can carry on taking mortgages.' Thousands of people were plunged into debt on a massive scale. Banks were prepared to finance your house, car and holidays for the same price. Thousands of people who had never aspired to so much, started to think about divine justice. The only mistake they made was trusting in the people seated in offices who were telling them there was no problem. The day would come when those same men in their pristine suits and ties would accuse those same people of living beyond their means.

An illusion.

And the debt began to grow.

Only a few people saw the catastrophe coming before it actually hit. From their offices on the major avenues of big cities, the big men of the Wanstein Club bet on the fall, as they watched middle-class dreams rise like inflatable castles of debt.

And they won.

Light.

Darkness.

Today, sometime after that big crisis, history is repeating itself. 'Europe is recovering'. 'Greece will resist'. 'Spanish debt is stable'.

'The euro is rising to unprecedented levels above the dollar'. But amid this maelstrom of satisfaction and euphoria, the five members of the Wanstein Club have stopped making investments. The money that had, until then, been earmarked for buying euros via foreign businesses, has stopped coming. Privileged information or distorted information? Candela can feel Warnes's lopsided smile following her movements.

TICK-TOCK TICK-TOCK TICK-TOCK TICK-TOCK

Stuck behind a metal-barred gate, like the ones you see in old-fashioned jails, Candela asks herself what they were thinking.

'Did they think we mere mortals couldn't see? Or rather, what did they do to hide this from the rest of us?'

The rusty bars were wide enough to fit an arm between them. A dungeon? Is it the end? No. Candela spots a crank handle at waist height, indicating to her that the game will continue. Turn, turn, turn. Then in the other direction. Turn, turn, turn. Nothing happens. She needs more information.

She looks carefully and finally finds it. In the upper section of the gate, almost hidden by the rust, Candela makes out some numbers engraved on a metal plate.

She refuses to accept that history is repeating itself. This is why she has to reach the centre of the Daedalus and find proof that the Wanstein Club is manipulating the markets. She'll only be able to stop them if she can prove that what they are doing is illegal. She has 40 minutes left. Candela is not about to let millions of people get swallowed up by the illusion. Their only mistake in life has been to want a slightly happier life. She looks at the gate. She leaves her shoes on the floor and gets to work.

'I'm going to get out of here, Warnes. If you want to kill me, you'll have to do it yourself. Because I'm going to get to the end and I'm going to get the proof. I'll stop you.'

TO FIND THE CODE LOWER THE
HANDLE BY THREE POSITIONS

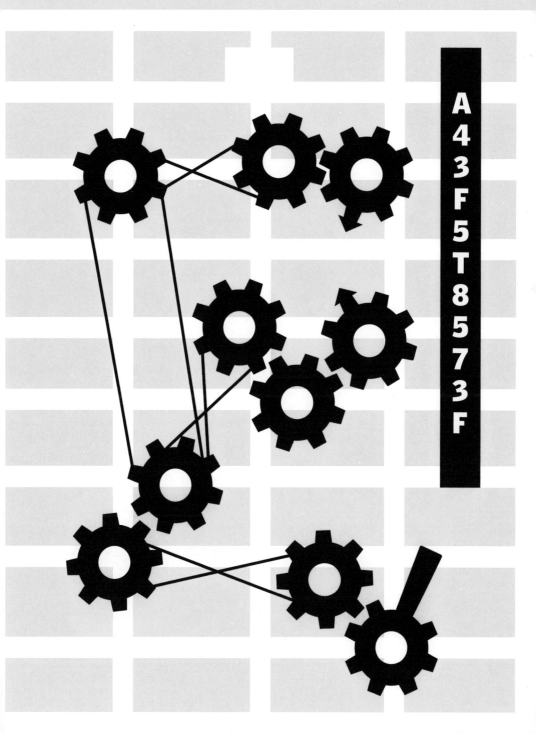

A43F5T8573F

On this page, the puzzle still hasn't been solved.
Find the code to know where to continue.
If you need to, consult the clues on page 147.
Write the code here so you can remember it later on.

CANDELA SOLVES THE GOLDEN-CUBE PUZZLE

She has 22 minutes left to live.

TICK-TOCK TICK-TOCK TICK-TOCK TICK-TOCK

With determination, Candela inputs the number sequence. She hears the noise of a motor and steps back. At knee-level, a section of one face of the cube disappears into thin air, as if it had been consumed by a hungry mouth. Candela doesn't give it a second thought and quickly goes through the opening – there's no time to lose. The opening closes behind her, as if by magic. She finds herself locked in a golden mausoleum measuring six by six metres. She looks up: there is no roof and the light from one of the big bohemian lamps is cast into the opening, allowing her to see.

'Art Room.'

Now she understands. Candela can see a painting and four apparently empty frames. They are hanging on the walls of this golden cube. She never judges things at face value, so she looks closely and discovers that some of these frames have numerical keypads below them. One of them is on the right-hand wall, underneath the solitary empty frame. The other three frames are on the opposite wall. The one in the centre has a numerical keypad underneath it, too.

But what draws Candela's attention is the abstract painting on the left-hand wall. That also has a numerical keypad.

It isn't a work of art by one of the so-called greats, it's just a mixture of blacks and yellows that doesn't mean anything to her. She looks at it determinedly, but cannot find any clues. It's starting to make her vision go blurry. Her head is numb, probably due to the poison, and she is having trouble thinking straight. She has 21 minutes left.

TICK-TOCK TICK-TOCK TICK-TOCK TICK-TOCK

Tomorrow, the newspapers will praise Castian Warnes for his generosity. The magnate who donated his castle and money to a good cause. They'll talk about the menu and the clothes. They'll show pictures of the rich and famous, posing at the entrance of his mansion. But they won't say that at one point in the evening, when everyone had consumed several glasses of happiness, the five members of the Wanstein Club had discreetly slipped away. They went off to finalise the details of the biggest attack on the financial world in history.

Several weeks earlier, the club had sold all of its corporate bonds. The market was catching up, so they had put them on the market at a good price. But they had sold so many of them that, in the end, the cost of the bonds had gone down. Supply had outstripped demand. They didn't care. They had already placed their bonds at a set price in the market, guaranteed by an underwriter.

Several days after that, the Wanstein Club had begun buying back its bond debt for less than the price at which it had sold it. The club had subsequently made a huge sum for this transaction.

But Candela knows that Warnes won't stop at buying thousands of euros. He'll want more. He'll want it all. If the Wanstein Club had been stopped at this point, Candela would have had to give up owing to lack of proof. But she knows that Operation White Bull is about much more than this, and it is still not over. The repurchase of bonds is no more than the next step in the plan. The Wanstein Club keeps taking steps to ruin Europe.

TICK-TOCK TICK-TOCK TICK-TOCK TICK-TOCK

'Come on, Candela! Wake up!'

Bang!

Two hands hit the wall. It hurts, and the pain freezes reality. She looks at her watch: 20 minutes. Bang. Another blow, more pain. She looks at her watch: 20 minutes. Candela pulls herself together. She has to carry on and get out of the Daedalus alive. What's more, she needs irrefutable proof about Operation White Bull. And she needs it before the European markets open. Bang. In five days' time, it will be the anniversary of black Wednesday; that's when the Wanstein Club will administer the final blow, Candela is sure of it. That's the day on which Operation White Bull will come to an end, ruining millions of families' lives.

For now, the only weapon within her grasp is a painting hanging on the wall within a golden cube without a ceiling. Her vision goes, her eyes cloud over. She holds her breath.

Bang.

Another blow. More pain. Candela wakes up.

Now she knows how to solve the puzzle.

On this page, the puzzle still hasn't been solved.
Find the code to know where to continue.
If you need to, consult the clues on page 155.
Write the code here so you can remember it later on.

CANDELA SOLVES THE FOOTPRINT PUZZLE

She has 30 minutes left to live.

TICK-TOCK TICK-TOCK TICK-TOCK TICK-TOCK

Candela inputs the footprint code and the door at the end of the tunnel opens. The music continues to play behind her. Candela looks behind and then looks ahead at the new space. It is different. Metal walls, metal ceiling, metal floor. A cube measuring just under one metre squared. A fluorescent light about two metres long is embedded into the ceiling and illuminates the space. Candela comes in without touching anything. The door closes behind her. Silence.

'It's just you and me now, Warnes.'

Candela memorises her surroundings. Every second counts. Behind her, the door that she came in by. To her left, there is a sticker with black stripes screen-printed onto it. To her right, a numerical keypad with the numbers in a single vertical line. On the wall opposite, her reflection looms, deformed in the steel as in a hall of mirrors.

'A lift. I'm in a lift!'

Certain that this has a special meaning, up, down, up, Candela looks at the numbers. She moves her index finger over the buttons and presses one at random.

Click!

Her heart is in her mouth as the lift descends rapidly. She instinctively holds out her arms and puts her hands on the walls to cushion her fall. Zooooom. Will it crash?

TICK-TOCK TICK-TOCK TICK-TOCK TICK-TOCK

The crash will come. If the Wanstein Club achieves its objective of breaking the euro, the crash will come. This will happen even if the majority of people don't know where it has come from. The emergency services that didn't arrive will never arrive. Salaries, which have been at their lowest for a long time, will continue to go down. State education will become more and more scarce. The crash will come. Every day, people will suffer the consequences. Meanwhile, the Wanstein Club will get away scot-free.

Although he appears to have forgotten it, Castian Warnes used to be an underdog. Now he is one of the top dogs. Up, down. That's how life goes. All you need to know is which button to press.

Following the death of his parents, 11-year-old Castian had fled from Albania with nothing. He had boarded a boat heading to France. There, he had learnt the little that was left for him to learn about poverty, abuse and ill-treatment.

Days later, the boat reached the port of Marseille. Castian disembarked, took one look behind him, then spat on the floor. He swore he would never be like the idiots who had treated him worse than an animal. And against all odds, Castian Warnes, the Albanian orphan, had gone on to become one of the most powerful men in the world.

TICK-TOCK TICK-TOCK TICK-TOCK TICK-TOCK

Zooooom.

Click.

The lift stops. Candela's stomach nearly leaps out of her mouth. The doors do not open and the fluorescent light blinks gently. She tries to avoid the fear that has crept underneath her skin. She is not feeling well; the poison has stunned her. She's losing focus. She breathes. Her chest goes up, down, up. She has 29 minutes left.

Sickening fortunes are created at the expense of others, the poverty of others. Candela is certain that it really is as simple as that. She wants to shout, but she is not strong enough, so she tries to visualise Warnes. She can see his face, his hands, his eyes. Her chest goes up, down, up. Her batteries are recharged by feelings of rage, hunger and hate for everything that keeps him alive.

TICK-TOCK TICK-TOCK TICK-TOCK TICK-TOCK

When he was 18, Castian Warnes had been awarded the Jean Paul Abarnou Scholarship. This had allowed him to go to the United States to study economics at Princeton. They say that Castian arrived on campus with a suitcase containing two jumpers, a pair of trousers, four changes of underwear and a toothbrush. He carried it to the assigned room that he would share, according to tradition, with a student who was not on scholarship and was the son of one of the city's most influential families.

There were two beds in the room, one next to the window with natural light and an excellent view of the campus. The other was on the other side of the room, where the roof almost touched the floor. Unless you were careful, you would definitely bang your head any time you went near it.

Castian looked at the beds, then looked his roommate straight in the eyes and challenged him.

If the gardener's cat walks under the window tomorrow, it's yours. If he doesn't, it's mine.

His new roommate was shocked by the cheek of this kid in a second-hand coat. He was also aware that the cat came past this window at least a hundred times a day. The roommate agreed to the bet, and didn't tell the kid that scholarship students didn't get the right to choose.

The next day, to the puzzlement of that red-haired Catholic boy, the gardener's cat was found in the swimming pool. It had drowned. From that day on, the boy's life was linked to Castian. Today, he is one of the five members of the Wanstein Club.

Castian learnt that there was much to be gained by influencing end results. And he'll do it again if Candela does not succeed in stopping him.

TICK-TOCK TICK-TOCK TICK-TOCK TICK-TOCK

The lift has not started to move again. Candela is calmer now that she has stopped panting. She focuses on the present. She takes a closer look at her surroundings and homes in on the printed sticker, getting so close to it that she is almost touching it with her nose. One end of it is slightly unstuck. Candela grips the front of her skirt tightly and tears the fabric. She covers her hands with fabric strips in case the paper contains a toxic substance that could penetrate her skin. Using her right hand, she very carefully pulls off the sticker. She is sure she'll need the whole thing if she wants to get out of the lift alive.

'Are you going to allow her to die alone, Castian?'

A smile, a laugh, an angry madness overwhelms her. She moves her chin upwards and howls until her voice is hoarse. She has 28 minutes left to live.

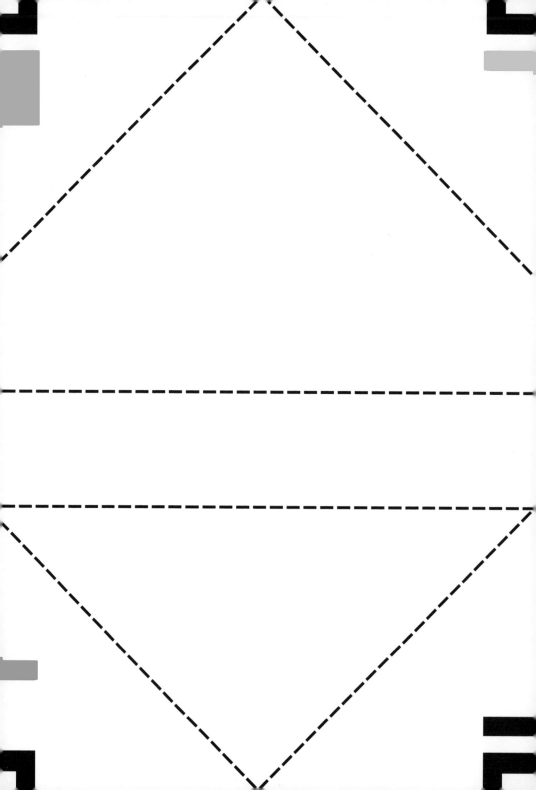

On this page, the puzzle still hasn't been solved.
Find the code to know where to continue.
If you need to, consult the clues on page 151.
Write the code here so you can remember it later on.

CANDELA SOLVES THE LIFT PUZZLE

She has 26 minutes left to live.

TICK-TOCK TICK-TOCK TICK-TOCK TICK-TOCK

When she folds the sticker in certain places, Candela finds a code. She taps it into the keypad and the lift goes down a bit more. Zooooom. Click. It stops again. Once again, fear. But this time, the doors open. Candela holds her breath. After each challenge, she has become accustomed to finding herself in impersonal grey and menacing anodyne spaces. The sight that now meets her eyes makes her think that she has reached the end of the Daedalus. But she is wrong: there are 26 minutes left.

Gold. Everywhere.

The space that opens up in front of Candela is both painful and astonishing. The room is huge and completely empty, apart from an enormous cube in the middle. Gold. Even though the room is gigantic, it is lit by the reflection of the light on the beautiful metal cube. Bohemian lamps, hung at two-metre intervals, project light, which then reflects off the cube and manifests as in thousands of bright stars. Candela counts 10 of these lamps from where she's standing. She approaches the cube, six square metres of shiny gold. Beyond it there are no doors, marks or life. Only the golden cube.

Candela touches the side of the cube with her fingertips. The quantity of wealth there hurts her. She's terrified because the person who has commissioned this room has crossed the final frontier of humanity, decency and reason. A visceral control overpowers everything.

Gold.

Candela doesn't know where to look. All she can do is walk around the cube feeling absolutely appalled. Gold. She closes her eyes. Gold. She keeps on walking. Gold. She shouldn't be surprised, she knew that Warnes was one of the wealthiest men in the world; but coming across so much fortune in one place has shaken her.

It's a simple rule.

If you want to make money, you need to have money in the first place. If you want to make some money, you need to have lots of money. If you want to make disgusting amounts of money, you need to have disgusting and blasphemous amounts of money.

Leading her to this room is Warnes' way of telling her that he's in charge. It's his game and she is going to play it. This room is Warnes' way of showing her who's boss.

'Run, Candela, run. There's not much time left.'

TICK-TOCK TICK-TOCK TICK-TOCK TICK-TOCK

Run, Candela. Over the past couple of months, this is what she has been telling herself each morning, when she has woken up to see that the Wanstein Club's plans have been coming to fruition, and she couldn't stop it. First, they bought euros. Then they started on the repo game.

Anyone can run a repo operation. It's essentially about trying to be a creditor. You leave your money in a bank so it has liquidity. In return, the bank pledges you a bond, which is actually public debt. The bank commits to repurchasing the bond for the same price, plus interest, within a specific time period. During this time, you can market, sell or repurchase the bond. Whatever you want. When the specific time period has elapsed, you give the bank a bond and the bank returns the investment to you, plus interest.

At the beginning, Candela asked herself why the Wanstein Club would want so many bonds of public debt from not particularly promising European countries. They were doing repos all over the world. Just that. Smoothly and slowly, via their front companies, so nobody would see. Then, when the Wanstein Club had a powerful enough position in the bond market, it started selling them. They didn't rush, but they didn't stop at any point, either. They saturated the bond market, and the price lowered accordingly. In turn, the risk premium went up, sowing seeds of mistrust.

The bond market and the currency market are separate, so the club members achieved their two objectives. Firstly, thanks to the large volume of currency purchasing taking place, the euro went up and up. Secondly, as a consequence of the bond selling, the risk premium skyrocketed. The perfect storm was brewing, and Candela could do nothing more than watch it helplessly, because even though she could sense what was happening, she could not prove it.

'I have to get into the Daedalus and find the proof before everything falls down.'

TICK-TOCK TICK-TOCK TICK-TOCK TICK-TOCK

Candela was walking around the golden cube. The first side, all gold. Turn. The second, all gold. Turn. The third, all gold. Turn. The fourth, also just gold, and two metres up, there was an inscription:

ART ROOM

Candela can imagine Warnes contemplating the golden cube like a pharaoh would his pyramid.

Above, an inscription. Below, a keyboard. Further down, lots of numbers and lines. A new challenge, a new test. Candela knows that Warnes will not be missing a single moment of the show, so she throws one of her hairclips into the air. Next, she leans her body against the wall of the cube. Tiredness is taking its toll.

She has 24 minutes left.

41 25 23 93 89 26 7 82 32

2

29

58 70 17 55 48 6 66

76 75 4 52 49 19 47 28

42 13 78 61 86 72 57 51 5

96 59 85 94 88 18 91

63 44 27 16

40 20 73 95

62 9 11 22 24 98 58 56

37

35 83 43 39 8 93

84 21 71 79 64 65

15 67 77 60 99 33 69

50 97 10

4 14 30 12 54 31 87 3

90 53 81 46 2 38

74 45 80 36

On this page, the puzzle still hasn't been solved.
Find the code to know where to continue.
If you need to, consult the clues on page 153.
Write the code here so you can remember it later on.

CANDELA SOLVES THE PUZZLE OF THE THREE PAINTINGS

She has 16 minutes left to live.

TICK-TOCK TICK-TOCK TICK-TOCK TICK-TOCK

The numbers hide behind the inky fabric in the same way that
Warnes hides behind his network of companies. Candela had
remained seated on the floor, but gets up as quickly as possible,
heading for the central painting. She walks towards the keyboard
beneath it so she can type in the code.

There's no time to lose. She only has 16 minutes left, and at
least one more puzzle to solve before she can get out of the cube.
One of the frames is still empty. Candela looks at it and sighs.

She inputs a code and prays for the 'click'. Now the third
painting shows its art.

TICK-TOCK TICK-TOCK TICK-TOCK TICK-TOCK

How many people would have got this far? Will Warnes really allow
her to keep moving forwards? Candela must not allow herself
to doubt, but she does. She doesn't want to be afraid, but she is
afraid. She needs proof, but doesn't have any. She needs the full
list of the companies they have used to make purchases, but it's
hidden. She needs the complete list of the businesses that will be
used later, but it's top secret. And if she wants to get hold of it, she
has to reach the end.

Candela remains imprisoned. If she tries to get out she will
have to keep playing the game, even though she may not want to.

Warnes and his club of very rich men are manipulating the
market. She knows it, but cannot prove it. Does he know? Candela
doubts it. At that moment, she remembers the photo in her living

room, of Warnes' face watching her from the centre of the map of drawing pins and thread. A photo of him chuckling. At her? Candela stops doubting. What she knows, she knows, even though she may not be able to prove it.

'Yet.'

TICK-TOCK TICK-TOCK TICK-TOCK TICK-TOCK

The painting is well lit by a chandelier. Candela looks at the painting. Its engraving is the same as all the others. The image, though different from previous ones, could be some kind of optical illusion. Candela repeats all the previous actions that have been successful. Eye-squinting. Nothing. Taking a few steps back. No number appears inside the frame.

'Lines on lines…'

One metre from the painting, Candela sighs. If she wants to survive, she has no choice. She will have to solve Warnes' puzzles. With 15 minutes remaining, she faces up to the next challenge.

On this page, the puzzle still hasn't been solved.
Find the code to know where to continue.
If you need to, consult the clues on page 159.
Write the code here so you can remember it later on.

CANDELA SOLVES THE PANEL PUZZLE

She has 3 minutes left to live.

TICK-TOCK TICK-TOCK TICK-TOCK TICK-TOCK

Candela is seated on the quilted sofa. As she inputs the numbers into the briefcase lock, cold sweat trickles down her back. She hears a 'click', which indicates that the combination is correct. She closes her eyes. She is tired, very tired, and if there is no antidote in the box, she will die in a couple of minutes. The last thing she will see is a dated room. She will be buried in the middle of the world, where no one will find her.

She opens the box. Inside, four syringes of different colours. Damn you, Warnes. Candela knows that only one of them contains the antidote. The others will kill her.

She has 3 minutes left to live, so Candela decides to inject herself with one of the vaccines. She knows she's out of luck. She only has a 25 percent chance of survival, but if she doesn't take the risk, then the odds will go down to zero. She chooses the yellow one, because it reminds her of the sun on the beaches she visited as a child. She pulls up one of her sleeves and positions the needle.

Riiiing, riiing…

The sound of the telephone makes Candela jump. The syringe falls on the floor, still intact.

She does her best to get to the phone and pick up the receiver. *The Blue Danube* plays in the background. She listens. In her head, the present blends with memories of the past. They, in turn, blend with fiction. Suddenly, she is standing on her father's shoes, dancing. But when she looks up, all she can see is Warnes's face, laughing loudly. Candela shakes her head. Maybe it's all a dream?

The music stops. Silence. A voice. It's him.

Every maze has a crossroads. You have the key, Candela.

Durrrrrrrrrrrrrrrrrrrrrrrrrrrrrrrrrrrrrrrrrrrrrrrrrrrrrrrrr. A single dial tone.

Candela lets the handset fall. She doesn't know if she is dreaming, if what she just heard is true, or if she has already got past the place where nothingness is the only refuge. On the stopwatch, it says 1 minute and 15 seconds.

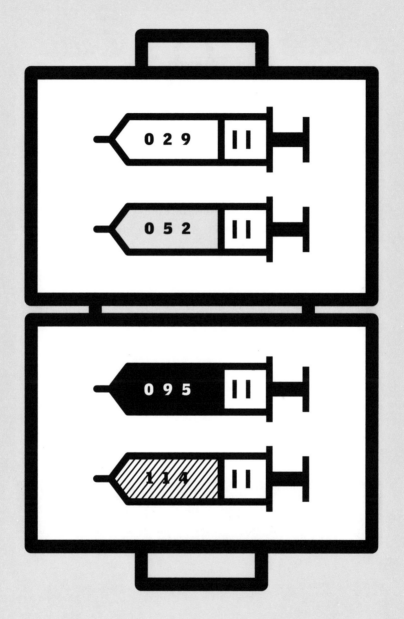

🔒

On this page, the puzzle still hasn't been solved.
Find the code to know where to continue.
If you need to, consult the clues on page 173.
Write the code here so you can remember it later on.

CANDELA SOLVES THE PUZZLE OF THE FIRST PAINTING

She has 19 minutes left to live.

TICK-TOCK TICK-TOCK TICK-TOCK TICK-TOCK

Candela finds herself in front of the abstract painting. A stereogram? It's one of those images you can only see clearly if you look at it with your eyes half-closed. Poison and blurry vision, that's the key. She finds three numbers that she inputs quickly into the keypad beneath the painting.

Beep, beep, beep.

Beep, beep, beep.

To her right now, is the wall with three empty frames. With a metallic sound, the same image appears within each of the frames. There are black triangles on a white background. Candela turns her head to see what it's about. Too quickly, her vision blurs again. So much gold, so much ostentatiousness. It's suffocating. Or maybe that's the poison. There's no way back now.

Candela doesn't want to die. She's scared. When she was a child and used to get into bed, she would chase away her fear by praying sweetly, the way children do.

'Dear God, please don't let anything bad happen to Mummy or Daddy. Or to Danny, my neighbour who is very handsome. Or to Nancy, my dolly.'

She was scared, so she asked. She used to ask, and she did not always get what she asked for, but kept asking anyway. And although the tears would initially run down like a toboggan-ride of pain, they always came to a sweet end. Now Candela is scared and she cries, but she does not ask. If she wants something, she knows that this time she will have to take it, even as the tears are falling from her cheeks. Candela is scared and doesn't know whether her fear makes her stronger or weaker. She only knows that she does not want to die. She is afraid of becoming nothing.

But she is still alive for now. Alive and lost in front of three paintings full of black triangles on a white background.

Still locked up.

Candela despairs. She needs to get out. If she does not find the code in the next few minutes, or even seconds, she will faint. She doesn't know how long she'll be able to last. And if she faints, the world as she knew it when she entered Ferulic Castle several hours ago will disappear for ever. Two or three generations condemned to misery for a handful of gold. And she will be dead.

She leans against the wall and breathes in air with her face stuck to the cold and precious metal. She breathes in once or twice. Her breathing has quickened; she needs to calm down and regain her balance.

'What are you doing here, Candela? What are you doing?'

She is looking for proof, to avoid disaster, to find the centre. To bring down Castian Warnes. Candela must reveal Operation White Bull at all costs. She lets out a scream of anger and strength, then calm returns to her body.

'You had no choice, you had to get into the Daedalus, my dear.'

It's her father's voice. Is she losing her mind? She only has 18 minutes left.

TICK-TOCK TICK-TOCK TICK-TOCK TICK-TOCK

The past few months have been very difficult for Candela. Every morning, she has sat down in front of her computer with a cup of coffee. She has been watching the Wanstein Club's movements, but hasn't been able to do anything to stop them. She has watched them buying euros with foreign currency. She has seen how increased demand made the euro go up in value. She has watched them do repos by lending money to banks in exchange for debt bonds. She has watched them inundate the bond market, bringing down the value of those bonds. She has then watched these bonds reach their risk levels and the club return to buy the same bonds days later for a much cheaper price. She has watched them return the bonds to the banks and recover costs. She has watched them charge interest and make money. Candela has watched all this, but has not been able to do anything. Millions and millions of euros in the hands of the Wanstein Club. And they kept on doing different things to make the plan take shape.

She knows them, she studies them, she gets their logic. She is sure. In five days' time, the Wanstein Club will activate the next phase of Operation White Bull and will bring down Europe. In a few hours, they will exchange all their euros for dollars, creating more supply than demand – so much more supply than demand. The euro will hit rock bottom.

By doing this via an infinite number of shell companies, it will be very difficult to detect that they have manipulated the markets in such a cold-blooded way. It will look like a knee-jerk reaction by small investors due to 'how badly things have been going in Europe' over the past few months, with risk premiums sky high. Falls in the premium that caused the Wanstein Club to sell bonds.

The wolves will wait until the euro has hit rock bottom and then they will start buying again, thereby going full circle. They know that, in reality, the euro is still strong and the fall is no more than a work of fiction. Little by little, the value of the European currency will go back up and Operation White Bull will be complete.

That is why she had no choice. She had to get into the Daedalus and stop this from happening. Or die trying.

That evening, Candela had put on her long, light-green and black skirt. She had painted her lips red, and had done the only thing left to do. Her big plan was to attend the gala and look for the entrance to the Daedalus, the biggest and most sophisticated safety-deposit box ever made, then inhale the poisonous gas and pray that the antidote actually existed. To find proof that the Wanstein Club is much more than an investment fund. Then, to get out alive and tell the world that five of the most powerful men in finance were salivating at the thought of ruining Europe.

It had felt right as she walked out of the editorial department. It had seemed necessary as she put on her tights. She had found it exciting as she walked into Ferulic Castle. It had seemed brave as she snuck into Warnes' study.

TICK-TOCK TICK-TOCK TICK-TOCK TICK-TOCK

Candela has now lost all her strength and is leaning against the wall. Once again, she rests her forehead against the cool gold surface. Her feet are wobbly. Her head hangs with exhaustion. She stretches her arms to keep her balance. She's shaky. She grits her teeth and her knees give way. She falls. She sits on the floor and looks up. Opposite, the three paintings appear to be mocking her. And with their laughter they show her the way.

Hidden in the paintings is a code. Her father showed it to her.

'Whenever there's a problem, distance yourself so you can see things clearly.'

Distance. That's the key. With her strength renewed, Candela uses it to deal with the grey-eyed devil.

On this page, the puzzle still hasn't been solved.
Find the code to know where to continue.
If you need to, consult the clues on page 157.
Write the code here so you can remember it later on.

CANDELA SOLVES THE PUZZLE OF THE ENGRAVINGS

She has 6 minutes left to live.

TICK-TOCK TICK-TOCK TICK-TOCK TICK-TOCK

With her legs buckling under the effort, Candela gets up, types in the code, and watches the door finally open. By now, her fingers have stopped responding to instructions, so she had to make several attempts. She knows she will not be able to manage much more of this. She gets ready to move on, but is petrified. Behind her lies the sobriety and uniformity of the maze. What now greets her makes her breathing falter. This is not the first time this has happened tonight. She is sure she has reached the end. What she doesn't know is what kind of an end it will be. Will it be the one that awaits the screen heroine who is always saved in the nick of time? Or the real-life version, where it is so difficult for the good guys to win?

A Victorian room appears before her. This is where Castian Warnes has his secret office. Unsteadily, she enters.

'I've made it!'

The walls are beige. To the left of the room, a big white rug is on a sofa. Two quilted armchairs with curved, mustard-coloured backrests are positioned around a marble table with edges of gold metal.

The lights are on. Floor lamps with lampshades that have claret -coloured flecks. They match the big velvet curtains that hang on the right side of the room. The curtains seem to cover three big panels. A beam of light seems to be filtered from behind them. The whole room embraces her in a very pleasant warmth, inviting her to recline on any of the chairs and simply relax.

Relax.

Sleep.

Die.

Her pulse quickens. Just in front of her, five computer screens take her by surprise. They blend in with the old-fashioned interior. Everything is elegant, not a single thing is out of place. It is the epitome of perfection and harmony, rolled into one.

A coughing fit has Candela bent double, then she falls onto the floor. She's now exhausted by the effort required of the past couple of minutes.

Relax.

Sleep.

Die.

'I need the antidote.'

She crawls to the table of computers and places her trembling hands on the edge of the table, stands up, and has a look at the table top. Computers, a silver tray with a letter opener, a half-open wooden box containing a fountain pen and a golden ballpoint pen. There's a vintage rotary dial telephone and... a metal briefcase labelled with the international biological hazard symbol.

The antidote. She has 5 minutes left. Candela can see the combination lock on the box.

She sobs. There isn't enough time. She can't do this anymore.

Relax.

Sleep.

Die.

She sobs in anger. She imagines Warnes laughing to himself as she crawls along.

Wake up.

Live.

With an anger that emerges from deep within, a feral scream fills the room, bringing Candela back to life.

'I. AM. NOT. GOING. TO. DIE!'

Candela takes the suitcase and examines it from top to bottom. She picks it up and sees an inscription.

LOOK FOR THE LIGHT

Light? Candela looks around. The lamps are switched off. She looks at the ceiling. She doesn't feel strong enough to get up and examine the exquisite bohemian light hanging from it. She falls onto the quilted sofa and sits with the briefcase on her lap, looking at the velvet curtains in front of her. In her mind, she goes over all the puzzles she has had to solve to get the middle of the Daedalus. Then she realises. The lift! It's impossible for natural light to get into it.

She tugs the curtain cord, and when they open, three huge panels full of numbers challenge her once again.

She doesn't even look at the stopwatch. She doesn't care about winning. What's important to her now is that she must not surrender.

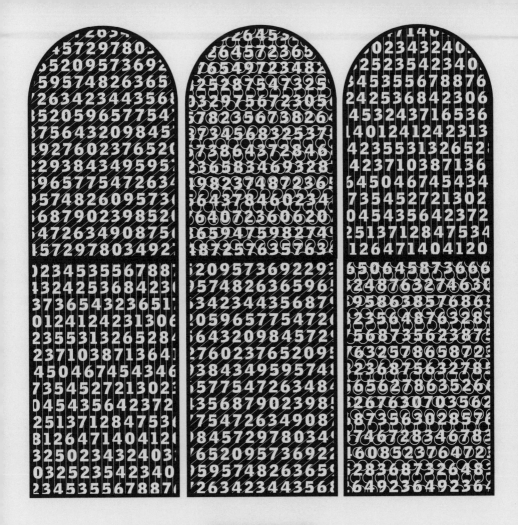

LOOK FOR THE LIGHT

On this page, the puzzle still hasn't been solved.
Find the code to know where to continue.
If you need to, consult the clues on page 171.
Write the code here so you can remember it later on.

CLUE ZONE

CLUE INDEX

Metal-plate puzzle

CLUE 1

The code lies in the bolts on the metal plates.

CLUE 2

On the big plate, some numbers are hidden.

CLUE 3

On the small plates, each group of bolt lines indicates the position of a hidden number.

CLUE 4

Look at the first group of bolt lines on the big plate and cover the rest. Repeat for the remaining groups of bolt lines.

CLUE 5

The order of the small plates is also the order of the code.

SOLUTION »

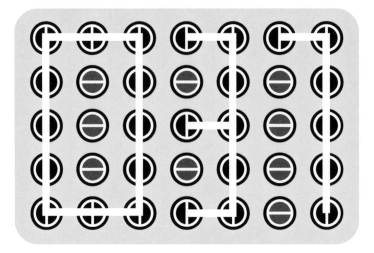

037

Mirror puzzle

CLUE 1

The code lies in the mirror.

CLUE 2

Look at the numbers in the reflection.

CLUE 3

Superimpose the lines on the mirrors on the reflected numbers.

CLUE 4

Look towards a light.

CLUE 5

On the superimposed image, you will find the code.

SOLUTION »

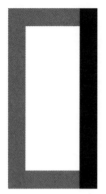

085

Metal-barred-gate puzzle

CLUE 1

The code lies in the inscription. To read it, imagine that the numbers are letters.

CLUE 2

As the inscription says, lower the lever by three positions.

CLUE 3

The cogs turn as you lower the lever, but not all in the same direction.

CLUE 4

The movement of the lever will also move the final cogs.

CLUE 5

The code is two numbers and reads from top to bottom.

SOLUTION »

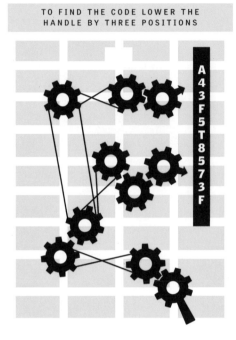

TO FIND THE CODE LOWER THE
HANDLE BY THREE POSITIONS

A43F5T8573F

47

Footprint puzzle

CLUE 1

The code lies in the number of toes visible on the footprints.

CLUE 2

The phrase 'the emphasis is the code' gives you a clue. But consider that it isn't only words that have emphases – music has them, too.

CLUE 3

The music playing is a waltz. The emphasis of the waltz goes in the first syllable of the compass: **1**, 2, 3, **1**, 2, 3, **1**, 2, 3.

CLUE 4

The code lies in the number of toes on the footprints that fall on the emphasis: the first of each group of three.

CLUE 5

The footprints appear in a tunnel, in line, one in front of the other. The order of the numbers in the code follows the order in which the footprints appear.

SOLUTION »

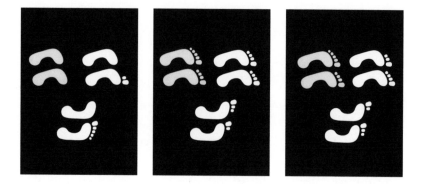

Lift puzzle

CLUE 1

The code lies in the shapes drawn on the sticker.

CLUE 2

The dotted lines indicate where you need to fold.

CLUE 3

Fold the paper until the shapes meet each other.

CLUE 4

You can fold backwards or forwards as you like.

CLUE 5

A three-digit number will appear.

SOLUTION »

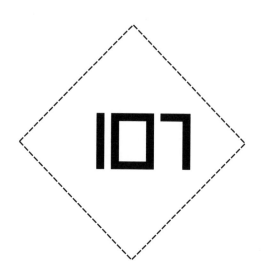

Golden-cube puzzle

CLUE 1
The code lies in the numbers.

CLUE 2
You need to find the distinguishing feature.

CLUE 3
Are all the numbers there? Do any repeat?

CLUE 4
Cross off the numbers so you don't lose count.

CLUE 5
There is a repeated number. That is the code.

SOLUTION »

93

Puzzle of the first painting

CLUE 1

The code lies in the painting.

CLUE 2

It's a stereogram – aka a magic-eye painting.

CLUE 3

Stereograms are seen by defocusing your view.

CLUE 4

Move away from the image.

CLUE 5

You will see a three-dimensional image in the top right area. That's the code.

SOLUTION »

125

Puzzle of the three paintings

CLUE 1

The code lies in the images in the paintings.

CLUE 2

You need to move back to see them clearly.

CLUE 3

Move away a few metres and look.

CLUE 4

You will see a hidden number in each painting.

CLUE 5

The order of the code is the order in which the numbers appear.

SOLUTION »

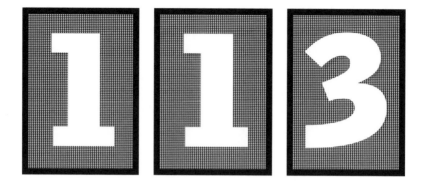

113

Puzzle of the final painting

CLUE 1

The code lies in the stripes of the painting.

CLUE 2

Not all stripes go in the same direction.

CLUE 3

You guess more than you can see.

CLUE 4

The stripes on the outside of the canvas frame the number.

CLUE 5

The code is a two-digit number.

SOLUTION »

17

Light-room puzzle

CLUE 1

The code lies in the phrase Castian said.

CLUE 2

He said *Find me.*

CLUE 3

Find something different amid the multitude of zeroes.

CLUE 4

Each page contains a single number that isn't zero.

CLUE 5

The order of the code reads from left to right.

SOLUTION »

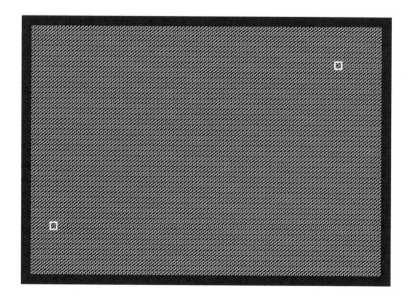

73

Letter-maze puzzle

CLUE 1

The code lies hidden in the letters of the word search.

CLUE 2

The hidden letters in the word search are next to each other. At the end of each word another begins.

CLUE 3

The words can go horizontally or vertically, but never diagonally.

CLUE 4

The first word you need to find is 'follow'.

CLUE 5

When you reach the three numbers, you'll have the code.

SOLUTION »

```
P F A D A L S M R T A C F O
W O R D R O D R R N D O M P
Z L A T E G O C U R S N H R
X T N D R I L D E J T E O
Y I S T O R I A P K R C D
N W T H E I T Y O R T U U A
A D C W E M L M P L Y B R R
K M A P R T Z W K O C E O
N O M M E J N A B V O D B
J A I P L I F O A S I T A
Q B P N R Z U W Z H X A L
Z P T Y T M B T S W I A W O
V U O D I S C Y S T R E S C
T R E G J L M O T X D P Y
W L W I L E A D W D O M P
Z C I C R E R O Z Z N H R
X U D U E E K P X E T E O
Y H E B D E U A Y R C D
N L N R T V I O N I U A
A D R H A P R A B R R
K M Z U E L N U K X E O
N O Y V A C V W M D B
J A L A Z E R J J E T A
Q B B I J A L Q Q S A L
Z P A D R G Q X E Z Z A W O
V U X O G S Z M N V V N Q C
```

Follow the path and you will find that the code is zero, two, three.

023

Colour-maze puzzle

CLUE 1

The code lies in the path.

CLUE 2

Start from the top on the left and follow the pattern of colours.

CLUE 3

The path isn't necessarily straight, but it cannot be diagonal. Find the subsequent colour that follows the pattern.

CLUE 4

Follow the path, even if the colours are above or below, repeating the pattern until you arrive at the numbers.

CLUE 5

The order of the code follows the order in which you pass through the numbered colours.

SOLUTION »

Number-maze puzzle

CLUE 1

The code lies in the maze. The text explains how to solve the puzzle – to read it you need to work backwards.

CLUE 2

You must find the logic to know which box to go to.

CLUE 3

There is only one adjacent box linked to your box. If you're in a yellow box with horizontal stripes, you can go to an adjacent box that is yellow or has horizontal stripes.

CLUE 4

The text says you need to add up the steps so, at each stage you have to find the numbers represented by question marks. Each box is worth the sum of its parts. If the box is yellow with horizontal stripes, its value is that of a yellow box plus that of a box with horizontal stripes.

CLUE 5

Add up the numbers you find on the way. At the end, you'll have the code.

SOLUTION »

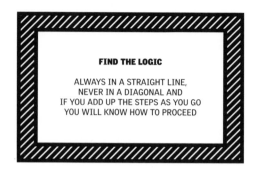

FIND THE LOGIC

ALWAYS IN A STRAIGHT LINE,
NEVER IN A DIAGONAL AND
IF YOU ADD UP THE STEPS AS YOU GO
YOU WILL KNOW HOW TO PROCEED

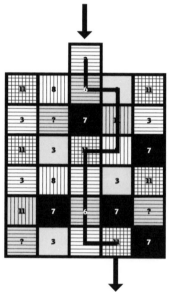

65

Puzzle of the engravings

CLUE 1

The code is hidden in the engravings.

CLUE 2

Everything depends on the viewing angle. Get level with the engraving and close one of your eyes. Look at the stretched letters in perspective.

CLUE 3

The hidden text is about elements and colours. You also have elements and colours in the door, where each drawing represents an element: water, earth, air and fire.

CLUE 4

Triangle pointing up with a line through it: air. Triangle pointing down: water. Triangle pointing up: fire. Triangle pointing down with a line through it: earth.

CLUE 5

Select each colour's element as indicated to get the code. The order follows that of the engravings.

SOLUTION »

white one is water
yellow one is fire
striped one is air

135

Panel puzzle

CLUE 1
The code lies in the numbers within the panels.

CLUE 2
Find the singularity. Are all numbers present within each of the six panels?

CLUE 3
The missing number in each panel will give you part of the code.

CLUE 4
Behind the numbers is a pattern.

CLUE 5
Follow the symbols on the briefcase to find the code.

SOLUTION »

119

Telephone puzzle

CLUE 1

The code is in the phrase Castian said: 'You have the key, Candela'.

CLUE 2

'You' is the key that will help you to solve the puzzle.

CLUE 3

On the telephone, there are letters corresponding to numbers.

CLUE 4

Transform the letters into numbers counter-clockwise.

CLUE 5

The code is in the correct syringe.

SOLUTION »

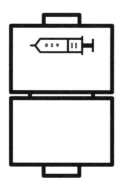

Computer puzzle

CLUE 1

The code lies in the word *answer*.

CLUE 2

You know the code has seven digits or letters.

CLUE 3

Castian's ego is a clue, as is the word *answer*.

CLUE 4

The word *answer* is an anagram of *Warnes* and *Castian* is an anagram of *Satanic*.

CLUE 5

On the screen, there is a connection between numbers and letters. Convert *Satanic* to numbers. The numbers marked in yellow give you the code.

SOLUTION »

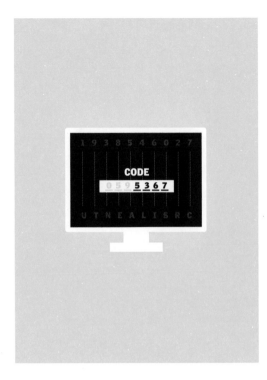